SO YOU'RE A

SPIRITUAL

BEING—

Now What?

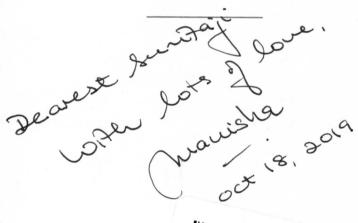

Dearest Smitaji

with lots of love,

Manisha

oct 18, 2019

PRAISE FOR SO YOU'RE A SPIRITUAL BEING —*NOW WHAT?*

"In this motivational and inspiring book, the author, Manisha Melwani, lays out a spiritual vision that integrates the physical, emotional, and the intellect guiding the reader to meaningful living, self-awareness, and greater happiness."

—Anita Moorjani, *New York Times* best-selling author of *Dying to Be Me* and *What If This Is Heaven*

"This book is a wonderful introduction for those curious about the path of spirituality. Even seekers who have started their journey will find many of their questions answered in simple and clear language, with many relevant examples from everyday life. Many books have attempted to explain spirituality but inevitably strayed from the teaching tradition. Manisha Melwani's book, *So You're a Spiritual Being—Now What?* stays true to the timeless wisdom of Vedanta, and for that I commend her. The book is presented in such a way that anyone can approach this book and benefit from the universally applicable knowledge."

—Swami Bodhatmananda, Resident Acharya, Vedanta Course, Sandeepany Sadhanalaya, Mumbai, India

"Although this book is based upon ancient teachings (Vedanta), it is a very clear and practical guide for living a full life today, or in any age. Manisha is a superb teacher, and that is evident throughout this book, as it is well written, easy to read, and incorporates many everyday examples and analogies, leading the reader gently to its various conclusions. I highly recommend this book to anyone who is looking to understand spirituality, and achieve purpose and balance in their lives. It provides readers with many easy-to-follow insights, definitions, and prescriptions for calming down and enjoying a life of more ease, fulfillment, and peace."

—Peter Dennis, M.B.A., Author, Speaker, Certified Consulting Hypnotist, www.peterhdennis.com

"Ms. Melwani has made a great effort to explain several essential concepts from the Vedanta approach to practical philosophy in a modern and easily accessible manner. Whatever one's age, experience, or background including prior readings might be, a motivated reader of this book is sure to find something of value to living life to its greatest potential."

—Dr. Ramesh Prasad, Professor of Medicine, University of Toronto, Ph.D. in Philosophy, University of Waterloo, Ontario

"A concise guide written with passion for readers, like me, who are fellow spiritual seekers! I gained insight from the intriguing answers that Manisha Melwani provides to pertinent questions she raises that I have raised myself. Manisha shares ancient teachings from masters in India with relatable case scenarios to illustrate the ancient teachings, making this stimulating book an easy read and engaging learning experience regardless of where you are on the spiritual path."

—Eleanor Silverberg, B.A. Psych, MSW, 3-A Coping Strategist, author of *Mindfulness Exercises for Dementia*

"Manisha Melwani does a tremendous job of addressing critical questions that have long overwhelmed seekers in a way the Western audience can study and appreciate. How does one grow spiritually? How do we become better people? To whom do we turn to for guidance? Based on the teachings of Swami Chinmayananda, founder of Chinmaya Mission, Melwani's work is perfect for all seekers on the path of spirituality, no matter their level. Everyone will find much to kindle their thinking in this book."

—Swami Advaitananda, Chinmaya Mission Nashik, Maharashtra, India

"Manisha takes esoteric spiritual knowledge, and grounds it in everyday life. Her book, *So You're a*

Spiritual Being—Now What? reminds us that the main purpose of life, even though we may have forgotten it, is to rediscover our spiritual essence. It gives us a well-designed, practical blueprint on what we must do to get there. This book is on par with many of the great spiritual books that I've read. I will definitely be reading it more than once as I continue on my own journey."

—Vasiliy Solodovnikov, Recovered Drug Addict & Alcoholic, Aspiring Author & Speaker, Devoted Spiritual Seeker

"This book sizzles with life! A must read for any of us, novice or seasoned, who want to embark on a rewarding spiritual journey! Manisha Melwani takes readers on a remarkable odyssey of discovery, humanity, realization, fulfillment, and much more. 'The truth is that real happiness isn't out there, but in here, within us.' This book provides a well-laid-out blueprint to begin, all you need to do is follow along, and make it your own! Read this book, and learn to walk and grow your own enriched, flourishing path."

—Roger Wheatley, Business Solutions Architect, www.BlogLogistics.com

"So You're a Spiritual Being—Now What? is an uncomplicated '101 course' in practical spirituality. It is accessible to any ardent spiritual seeker,

exploring any denominational spiritual path. It is a treasure trove of practical pointers that will serve as an exceptional resource. The fluidly articulated, strategic guidelines will surely serve as an easy access to an otherwise quite challenging (to absorb and digest) subject."

—Swamini Swaprabhananda, Resident Acharya, Chinmaya Mission Kharghar, Navi Mumbai, India

"Manisha's book has given me knowledge, practical tips, and techniques for my inner journey and taken it to a whole new level. The examples and explanations are a great way to use this book as a manual for expanding my journey to connecting with Spirit."

—Stephanie Bedford, R.N., B.A., BNSc, CNCC(C)

"Manisha has a gift. Utilizing a friendly, conversational style, she has taken complex philosophical concepts from the Vedanta tradition of ancient India and expressed them in a simple and understandable manner for the Western reader. She has demonstrated that the wisdom that originated thousands of years ago is ageless and universally relevant today, as it was in the past. This book is a must read for any seeker of wisdom."

—Tony Murdock, M.A., Meditation Instructor, Hindu Religious History and Christian Studies, McMaster University, Ontario. www.towardstillness.com

SO YOU'RE A

SPIRITUAL

BEING—

Now What?

A Straightforward Guide to Understanding
and Growing in Your Spiritual Journey

MANISHA MELWANI

BALBOA
PRESS

A DIVISION OF HAY HOUSE

Balboa Press books may be ordered through
booksellers or by contacting:

Balboa Press
A Division of Hay House
1663 Liberty Drive
Bloomington, IN 47403
www.balboapress.com
1 (877) 407-4847

Because of the dynamic nature of the Internet, any web
addresses or links contained in this book may have changed
since publication and may no longer be valid. The views
expressed in this work are solely those of the author and do
not necessarily reflect the views of the publisher, and the
publisher hereby disclaims any responsibility for them.

The author of this book does not dispense medical advice or prescribe
the use of any technique as a form of treatment for physical, emotional,
or medical problems without the advice of a physician, either directly
or indirectly. The intent of the author is only to offer information
of a general nature to help you in your quest for emotional and
spiritual well-being. In the event you use any of the information in
this book for yourself, which is your constitutional right, the author
and the publisher assume no responsibility for your actions.

Print information available on the last page.

ISBN: 978-1-9822-2944-3 (sc)
ISBN: 978-1-9822-2942-9 (e)

Library of Congress Control Number: 2019943812

Balboa Press rev. date: 08/12/2019

With love and heartfelt gratitude to my guru,
Swami Chinmayananda

CONTENTS

PREFACE

Spirituality is becoming widespread and being sought out by people from all backgrounds and cultures. The growing popularity of yoga, meditation, spiritual retreats, self-help and personal empowerment books and programs, and self-professed gurus all point to this trend.

Along with all this, there has been much confusion about common spiritual concepts. Words such as *soul*, *spirit*, and *spiritual* are used and interpreted differently. For instance, what is my soul? Am I the soul or do I *have* a soul? If I am a soul, why are we called "spiritual beings" and not "soulful beings"? What's the difference between soul and spirit? Have you wondered what people mean when they say, "Tap into your spirit" and "Ask what your spirit is saying"? If I am a spiritual being, then who is the "I" who is asking "my" spirit?

You may have read or heard this quote by the

French philosopher Pierre Teilhard de Chardin: "We are not human beings having a spiritual experience. We are spiritual beings having a human experience." When I first heard it a few years ago, it felt surprisingly good.

Isn't it funny how once a new phrase or song catches your attention, you find others around you echoing it? As I heard this phrase quoted repeatedly by various teachers, speakers, and authors in the self-help, spiritual, and personal development field, I began to feel uneasy. I didn't hear any explanation of *why* we are spiritual beings, only that we are. I was eager for a better understanding of what these speakers and teachers meant.

Previously, my strong interest in New Age spirituality led me to readily accept most of what I read and heard. But then, I began to see things in the light of new knowledge. This new knowledge was Vedanta (pronounced vay-DHAAN-ta), a spiritual science that originates from an ancient wisdom tradition from India. Studying the spiritual truths taught by the Vedantic masters, I began to think more deeply and question what I had easily accepted before.

Wouldn't it be great if there was one clear set of definitions in the spiritual field so everyone who hears the words *soul* or *spirit* for instance, would know exactly what they mean? The understanding would be based on facts and not colored by religious beliefs or cultural upbringing. Vedanta provides that clarity.

Early one morning, as I sat quietly by myself, I took out my journal, turned to a fresh page and wrote the words "You're a spiritual being." Suddenly, a question popped into my mind: "Now what?" And with that came a barrage of other questions: "What is a spiritual being?" "What is spirit?" "What does it mean to *be* spiritual?" "As a spiritual being, what am I supposed to be doing?" "What is spiritual growth and the spiritual journey?" "Can we *prove* that we are spiritual beings?" My research into the answers as they are found in Vedanta eventually became some of the topics of this book.

I have learned Vedanta as it was taught by my guru, Swami Chinmayananda, and his disciples. He was an outstanding teacher with a masterful ability to break down complex concepts into simple ideas through examples from daily life and with humor. His method of teaching Vedanta is the bedrock of this book. I owe my utmost gratitude to him. Wherever I have mentioned "Gurudev," please know that I'm referring to Swami Chinmayananda. ("Gurudev" is a reverential way to address one's guru.)

My knowledge has come from about twenty

years of listening to the teachings directly from the mouths of teachers, through self-study, and personal reflection. Since 2003, I've been actively participating in Vedanta study groups and in 2008, I began taking structured online Vedanta courses provided by the Chinmaya International Foundation in India. I've also studied some simple Sanskrit, the ancient language in which the spiritual teachings are written.

As you read this book, I hope that you will see me as a fellow spiritual seeker who is sharing her learning with you. Whether you are new to the spiritual path, already a seasoned traveler, or just curious, my hope is that you'll get a fresh viewpoint and gather some practical tools and tips to take on your personal journey.

ACKNOWLEDGMENTS

I owe my deepest gratitude to my guru, Swami Chinmayananda, who has been the source of endless inspiration and guidance in writing this book. Even though you are not physically here with me, Gurudev, you have stayed true to your promise, "Whenever you need me, close your eyes and look into your heart—and I will be there!"

I am profoundly touched by the ready support and blessings for this book from Swami Tejomayananda, Gurudev's foremost disciple and global head of the Chinmaya Mission (1993–2017). He also personally looked over chapter 2. Thank you so much, Guruji! Words cannot convey my feelings of love and appreciation for you.

I would also like to express my sincere gratitude to Swami Bodhatmananda, Swami Advaitananda, Swami Advayananda, and Swamini Swaprabhananda of the Chinmaya Mission. They have reviewed various chapters in this book to ensure that I have expressed the facts accurately. Their help and guidance have been an invaluable source of strength and confidence for me.

A special "thank-you" goes to my husband, Kumar, for giving me the idea to write a book, several years ago. He had faith in me and saw my potential to be a writer even before I did. He has been my rock and a wonderful support for all that I do.

I would like to thank my dear friend, Debra Flanagan, for using her fine copyediting skills to review and edit two versions of the manuscript. Debra, my sons Praveer, Devesh, and Arun Melwani, my daughter-in-law, Akansha Agrawal, and my niece, Sheena Melwani, gave me valuable direction in the initial and final stages of the manuscript and the book cover design. Their help ensured that the ideas in this book are presented well and are easy to understand.

I am grateful to my family and friends around the world who reviewed one or more chapters of the book and provided their helpful ideas and suggestions. Thank you so much: Kanta Melwani, Sarika Agrawal, Grettal Fryszberg, Nava Israel, Ranu Ramraj, Marsha Permut, Preeti Thadani, Padu Melwani Mahtani, Anita Raj Daswani, Vinita Sani, Nirmal Chawla, Michael Shuster, Ravindaran KPM,

Kishen Ravindaran, Caroline Lim, Tarvinder Kaur, Chand Mahtani and Sunny Mahtani. I am touched by their sincere desire to help me.

Manisha Khemlani, chief operating officer of the Central Chinmaya Mission Trust in Mumbai, India and her team were exceptionally prompt and professional in guiding me to meet the legal and design permissions required for this book. It was a pleasure working with them.

Lastly, I'd like to thank Paula Ann Dragosh, my final editor, for her expertise in ensuring the manuscript was cleaned up and ready to go to print. She was friendly, patient, and professional in her approach.

I am grateful and honored to have so much love and support in my life. I feel truly blessed.

INTRODUCTION

Vedanta is a *shastra*, a Sanskrit word meaning "science." A *shastra*, like any science, is a systematically organized, comprehensive body of knowledge on a particular field of study. It provides concepts, definitions, and explanations. Examples of sciences are biology, physics, chemistry, and astronomy. The field of study in Vedanta is spirit or the Self—the truth of who we really are, and the Ultimate Reality of the world.

If Vedanta is new to you, you may find that some concepts in this book are different from, and perhaps even contrary to, your knowledge of spirituality. For instance, you may have a differing opinion about the purpose of life (chapter 1, 3, 5 and 6), or that we live many lives (chapter 3 and 5). My intention is not to try to change your thoughts about these concepts but to simply present what Vedanta has to say about them. Some of these ideas echo what you may know or have heard about Hinduism. This is because Hinduism derives many of its teachings from the ageless spiritual writings of the _Vedas_ in which Vedanta is found. (You can read about the _Vedas_ and Vedanta in chapter 6.) The Hindu scriptures called the _Upanishads_ and the _Bhagavad Gita_ are considered to be authentic sources of Vedanta. These, along with other Hindu texts, have been used to reference Vedantic facts in this book because this is where those ideas are found. This does not in any way make the ideas limited or religious. They remain fundamental spiritual truths, usable and relevant to everyone.

I have not shied away from using the word _God_ (Chapter 2 and 9). I realize that it evokes different ideas and emotions in people. But considering this is a book on spirituality, I couldn't avoid using the term. After all, God is intrinsic to the topic, being the "spirit" in "spirit-ual" and "spirit-uality." If you are not comfortable with the word _God_, feel free to substitute it with another term for the Ultimate Cause of this world. I've presented the Vedantic explanation of God in chapters 2 and 5. Please take note of the various synonyms used there such as the _Self, Supreme Reality, Truth, Supreme Consciousness_ and _Om_. As you read this book, this will help you understand that the various terms all refer to the same thing.

Vedanta talks about the importance of cultivating devotion to God or the Supreme Truth to be able to attain it. I'm Hindu, and so I've presented the Hindu perspective of ways to develop divine devotion (chapter 9). Again, this is not to try to change your faith or understanding, but to simply share a perspective. You'll probably find that the methods to develop devotion are similar to your own faith and other faiths.

How to Use This Book

I've divided the content of this book into two main themes, as indicated in the title, "So You're a Spiritual Being" and "Now What?" In part 1, "So You're a Spiritual Being: Understanding the Basics," I present fundamental concepts about spirit, spirituality, being spiritual, and the spiritual journey. In part 2, "Now What?—How to Live as a Spiritual Being," I describe the habits, practices, and lifestyle of a spiritual seeker.

If you'd like some additional tools to help you implement this new learning into your life, you can download a free copy of *The Now What Workbook* at www.ManishaMelwani.com/the-now-what-workbook/ It would be best if you started on the workbook after you finish reading this book.

If you are curious to know more about Vedanta,

you may want to start your reading with chapter 6, "Vedanta." To get the most out of this book, read all the chapters in part 1 before moving on to part 2.

In the appendix, I've included a biography of Swami Chinmayananda, a narrative on how I met him and resources for further reading.

I'm excited about being a part of your spiritual journey! I've presented the topics as simply as I can. Thanks to the clarity of Swami Chinmayananda's teaching style, this wasn't too hard to do.

PART 1

So You're a Spiritual Being

Understanding the Basics

The spiritual path is not a journey in time and place. It is a movement in consciousness.
—Swami Chinmayananda,
Talks on Sankara's Vivekachudamani

CHAPTER 1

Understanding What It Means to Be Spiritual

Spiritual life is all-inclusive. A mere part effort with one aspect of your personality is not good enough to register progress. Your physical, psychological, and intellectual involvement is unavoidable.

—*Swami Chinmayananda,*
The Penguin Swami Chinmayananda Reader

You Eat Organic, Do Yoga, and Meditate— Are You Spiritual?

I f you say that you are spiritual, have you stopped to ask yourself why you think so? Is it about the kinds of activities and practices that you engage in? Does it have to do with how you see your life? What are the principles that you live by? As a spiritual being, what are you supposed to be doing, and *why*? What is your real purpose?

To answer these questions, it may be a good

idea to begin by recalling what brought you to the spiritual path in the first place. The truth is, most of us don't turn to spirituality unless there is a reason to do so. Changes and challenges in relationships, circumstances, or health often spur us to seek spiritual solutions. Remembering why you chose spirituality could give you a clearer understanding of why you're doing what you do now, what sustains your interest and commitment on the path, and your primary spiritual goal.

The story of Lori in this chapter may help you gain a better appreciation of what it means to be spiritual, and answer a few of your questions too.[1] As you read her story, you may find some similarities with your own . . .

Picture Lori, a petite and energetic thirty-two-year-old insurance broker whose entire life revolved around her work. Ambitious and determined, she set aggressive goals and pushed herself to achieve them by meeting clients after work every day, and even on weekends. She lived alone and had a handful of close friends whom she had known since high school. They often invited her out for movies, meals, and other get-togethers, but she wasn't able to join them most of the time. She was always busy meeting clients or working on her computer to find them the

---

[1] All the characters in this story are fictional.

best insurance deals. She loved helping people and was very successful at her job. Her drive, diligence, and professionalism brought her a constant stream of new clients. Although selling insurance wasn't her real passion, the money was good, so she stuck with it.

Lori had an older sister, Kathy, whom she hardly saw. Kathy was a stay-at-home mom with twin boys who loved playing sports. They kept her busy driving them to various practices and games before and after school. Unlike Lori, Kathy was very close to their mother, Mona. Mona was a seamstress who had always had a taste for the finer things in life such as fashionable clothes and fancy jewelry. She and her husband ran a small dry cleaning business, where she offered tailoring and alteration services. The hours were long and the profits, modest. When Kathy and Lori were twelve and eight, their father died in a car accident, leaving his family with very little savings. Mona had to manage the business while bringing up her daughters on her own. She dreamed about the time when she could sit back and enjoy a comfortable retirement.

When the girls grew older, they found part-time jobs. Kathy worked at a clothing store at the mall, and Lori, who was always very creative, worked at Mona's sister's flower shop. Lori loved using her hands to create beautiful flower arrangements and was a natural at it. The customers admired her designs and asked for her whenever they needed flowers. When she was thirteen, Lori dreamed about running her own flower shop one day.

Kathy got married when she was only twenty-two. Her husband was a young, tech-savvy CEO of a successful startup company. Suddenly, Kathy became her mother's pet. She was the perfect daughter living the wealthy lifestyle that Mona had always wanted for herself. Kathy showered her mother with gifts and gave her diamond jewelry for her birthday and on Christmas. When the twins were born, Mona happily sold her dry-cleaning business to help Kathy take care of them. Kathy took her mother with her family when they went on various trips to the Far East, Europe, and Hawai'i. Lori was sidelined and left to herself. She was either studying or working. As the years went by, she met her mother and her sister less and less frequently.

Lori felt bitter about her mother's neglect and was secretly jealous of Kathy. The two sisters had always been very different. Kathy was the charmer and popular girl, whereas Lori, like her father, was more introverted and hardworking. Seeing her mother dote on Kathy made Lori feel determined to prove herself to her mom. She paid her way through college by tutoring other students and waiting on tables at an upscale restaurant where she earned generous tips. When she graduated with her business degree, she worked a few different jobs before settling on selling insurance.

After five years, long working hours and rising stress levels were wearing her down. She started getting frequent headaches, developed digestive issues, and suffered from a bad back. She found it increasingly difficult to focus on her work. Lori realized that she needed to slow down and take better care of herself.

On her way home every day, she would walk past a small yoga studio a block from her subway stop. She saw many women going in and out of the busy little studio and often thought of popping in to see what the place was like. One day, she noticed a big sign outside the studio: "Join now and get 50% off a 12-month membership! Try out a free yoga class today!" She thought, "Wow! That's a great offer." Impulsively, she walked in. A friendly young woman greeted her and showed her around. Lori liked what she saw and registered for a free class the coming Saturday. She had never done yoga before and was excited to try it out.

Lori's introductory yoga class was for beginners, so they did only gentle stretches and breathing exercises. Nevertheless, she was surprised and delighted at how much more relaxed mentally and physically she felt afterward. When an employee of the studio asked her if she would like to take advantage of the discounted fees and sign up for a yearly membership, she readily agreed.

Lori began to leave work early three times a week to attend yoga classes. Soon, her headaches started to diminish, and her back wasn't as sore anymore. Doing yoga also made her more open to other holistic practices. She heard that meditation could help her relax and balance her emotions. So she joined a meditation class at the studio.

Her meditation teacher was a vegan who recommended a vegetarian diet for a healthier body and mind. Lori thought that it sounded like a good idea, especially since her digestive issues had not resolved with the medication that her family doctor had prescribed. She cut back on her meat consumption and joined a vegetarian cooking class offered in her community.

At the class, she met someone who told her about a doctor who combined conventional medicine with Traditional Chinese Medicine in his practice. Lori decided to visit him. He diagnosed her problem and treated her with acupuncture and Chinese herbs. He introduced her to a nutritionist who guided her to make more changes to her diet. She started eating mostly organic, whole foods and taking natural supplements. All this vastly improved her health.

Lori was more empowered with her new life choices than ever before. She felt a strong urge to continue to learn and grow. She made new friends with three women who attended classes at the yoga studio. Together, they explored various vibrational, healing, and New Age practices. They used flower essences and crystals to open the special energy centers in their bodies called chakras. They used angel oracle cards to access guidance from their angels. They also tapped into their own intuition by learning how to interpret the movements of a special pendulum, a semiprecious stone hanging from a short metal chain. When the women understood that thoughts have the power to manifest their desires, they used positive statements called affirmations to assert and achieve their goals. Finally, they also got training in Reiki, a technique of channeling energy through the hands to reduce stress and promote healing. Lori was thoroughly enjoying the new learning.

It's not unusual to find that when people start looking into unconventional practices such as these, they discover a whole new world waiting to be explored. Naturally, they are curious and experiment with many things like Lori did.

Considering that Lori had made changes to her diet and lifestyle, and embraced the new mystical and healing practices, would you say that she was now spiritual? In other words, does eating organic foods, doing yoga, meditating, and adopting New Age practices make you spiritual?

Being spiritual isn't only about what you *do*; it begins with how you *see* your life. Your vision then guides your actions.

Holistic Is Spiritual

Vedanta asserts that all of creation is permeated by one spiritual essence.[2] Although outwardly there appear to be differences or separation between objects and beings, intrinsically, there are none. All are different expressions of one spirit. This truth of oneness is the highest spiritual truth.

The physical body is a good example to explain this principle of oneness. All the various parts are different from each other and perform their own individual functions. However, your vision of who you are encompasses your whole body. If someone taps your shoulder or back, you naturally turn around to see what he or she wants. You consider all parts of your body as one "you."[3]

---

[2] Chinmayananda, *Ishavasya Upanishad,* verse 1, 68.

[3] Tejomayananda, *Right Thinking,* 11.

The principle of oneness underlies a holistic view of life. You understand that your choices and actions in one area affect your whole life. Therefore, when you take a holistic approach, you are actually adopting a spiritual view. In Lori's case, she realized that her focus on work meant that other areas of her life were suffering. She saw that things would become worse unless she took some steps to remedy the situation. She took charge of her overall health by choosing yoga, meditation, and better eating habits. In adopting holistic solutions, she was embarking on her spiritual path. This was the beginning of her inner transformation.

Growing Spiritually

As she reflected on her life, Lori realized that she had placed material goals ahead of her passion. She thought back to her happy teenage years when she used to work at her aunt's flower shop. She remembered how she had wanted to own her own flower shop one day. As the years rolled by though, the desire to prove to her mother that she was capable of supporting herself with a good income had pushed her dreams far into the background. Selling insurance was not something that she had imagined herself doing with her life. She remembered the scent of the flowers on her hands and how happy it used to make her feel. The memory brought a deep sadness at the core of her being. She regretted the lost time and the opportunities she never explored.

Lori experienced a deep shift within herself. She felt that she couldn't wait any longer to pursue her passion. She quit her job and found another one at a floral boutique. She was not earning anywhere near what she used to when she sold insurance, but she was much happier. Luckily, she had built herself a good nest egg through hard work and smart investments in her old job. She enrolled in a part-time floral design program at a vocational institute and was on her way to living her dreams. She felt more alive than she had in years. She was confident that she would be the proud owner of a flower shop one day.

As Lori began living in alignment with her true self, she reconnected with her high school friends, and they met often. Being with them grounded her and made her feel happy and safe. She began to exude an inner glow. She caught the attention of Rick, a friend of one of her old friends. He was kind, jovial, and a genuinely nice man. They hit it off and started dating.

As Lori's life brightened up, her commitment to her spiritual path deepened. She reflected on the aspects of her personality and habits that she could improve. She took to heart the Golden Rule: *Do unto others as you would have them do unto you.* Aside from the obvious fact that we should treat others well because this is how we ourselves want to be treated, the basis of this rule is the truth of our essential oneness with each other. Lori was aware of the fact that she could sometimes be a little blunt when she spoke with others. She promised herself that she would do her best to speak in a kind and pleasing manner. She practiced being friendly, accepting, and loving with others. To bring out the spiritual shine from within herself and to do more for others, she started to volunteer at the local food bank every week, and also helped at a soup kitchen feeding the homeless once a month.

She began expanding her spiritual knowledge of life. She started attending various seminars on spirituality and reading books on the topic. One of the first things she learned was that while science tells us that we are a species called *Homo sapiens,* spirituality declares that we are essentially pure spirit expressing in human form. After a few months, she joined a weekly Vedanta study group where serious spiritual seekers met to study and discuss spirituality. She started waking up early every morning for spiritual self-study and reflection followed by a focused meditation practice.

Her spiritual studies helped her understand the similarities in the underlying principles of all religions. She no longer doubted the existence of God. She started to occasionally attend services at the church where she used to go with her parents as she was growing up. Though she remained with her own Christian faith, she became open to all faiths. She attended meditation sessions at a nearby Buddhist temple and enjoyed participating in Hindu devotional chanting sessions known as *kirtans*.

One day, Lori felt the urge to mend her relationship with her mother and Kathy. She invited them out for lunch at the old pizzeria in the neighborhood where she and her sister grew up. She told them that she had something important to talk about. Surprised at her invitation and curious to hear what she had to say, Mona and Kathy agreed to meet her. Lori spoke from her heart. Regretfully, she admitted that she had resented her mother for spending more time with Kathy. And she confessed to Kathy that jealousy had made her stay away from her. They talked openly for over three hours.

Mona was moved by her daughter's love and sincerity. She realized her own shortcomings and apologized to Lori for not being sensitive to her needs.

Kathy admitted that she had been so preoccupied with her family life that she hadn't made the effort to include Lori. The three ladies hugged each other as tears flowed down their cheeks. They felt a closeness they had never shared before.

In five years, Lori became a totally different person. Her initial commitment to taking a holistic approach in one aspect of her life gradually led to the transformation of her entire life—her physical, emotional, and mental health, her career and life path, her relationships, and her spiritual blossoming. She found a greater sense of peace and purpose and was happier than she had ever been in her life.

Being on the Path

Vedanta tells us that our true nature is different from the ever-changing and perishable aspects of our human personality—the body, the senses, the emotions, and the thinking mind.[4] We are essentially divine.[5] Our ultimate purpose is to rediscover this divine spiritual essence, also known as the Self. Right now, however, we don't know it.

Swami Advayananda, the lead teacher of Vedanta at the Chinmaya International Foundation in South

[4] Chinmayananda, *Atmabodha,* verse 18, 37.
[5] Chinmayananda, *Kindle Life,* 55.

India, has a series of three YouTube talks titled "Reaching the Self."[6] In the first one, he explains that we don't experience our spiritual nature because of three inherent defects in us. They are the veiling of the Self, and the impurities and restlessness of the mind.

The veiling of the Self. This veiling causes us to be ignorant of our true nature and to think of ourselves as limited individuals instead.

Impurities in the mind. These are desire and its resulting negative reactions—anger, greed, delusion, pride, and jealousy. They are collectively known as the *Six Enemies.* All other negative emotions are expressions of these six main impurities. Like all of us, Lori experienced the *Six Enemies* in her life. She had a *desire* to get her mother's love and attention. When she didn't get it, she became *angry* and began to think that she needed to make more money to earn it (*delusion*). Meanwhile, she felt *jealous* of Kathy, who was getting all the attention. Vedanta explains that when desire is thwarted, it leads to anger, delusion, and jealousy, as in Lori's case. But if desire is repeatedly fulfilled, it leads to *greed*, which also causes *delusion*. This delusion expresses as *pride* in one's possessions and brings up feelings of *jealousy* when others are perceived as having more.

---

[6] Advayananda, "Reaching the Self—Part 1."

Restlessness of the mind. This inner restlessness prevents us from having single-minded focus for spiritual study and practice.

The main defect is the veiling of our spiritual nature. It gives rise to the other two defects. Here's why: The Self is infinite, immortal, and blissful.[7] However, because we don't know or experience it, we take ourselves to be just the opposite—limited, mortal, and often sorrowful humans. In an unconscious effort to regain the fullness of our being, desires to fulfill ourselves arise. We turn to the world with the mistaken notion that it contains happiness in the form of things, people, and circumstances that we can enjoy.[8] Then, depending on whether we get what we desire, negative reactions such as anger, greed, delusion, pride, and jealousy crop up (the second defect). These impurities in turn create restlessness in the mind (the third defect).

Swami Advayananda explains that the veiling or ignorance of our spiritual nature can be removed only by gaining the knowledge of the Self. For Self-knowledge, a peaceful inner atmosphere has to be developed. This will naturally happen when the impurities and restlessness of the mind are cleared away.

---

[7] Chinmayananda, *Meditation and Life,* 32, 33.
[8] Chinmayananda, *Self-Unfoldment,* 41.

Lori reduced the impurities and restlessness in her mind by adopting holistic solutions for her health, doing work that expressed her innate nature, striving to live by the Golden Rule, volunteering in the community, developing her heart through religious and devotional practices, and reconciling with her family. She also started removing the veiling of the Self by attending a spiritual study group and by maintaining her daily self-study, reflection, and meditation.

By making the right choices and following up with the right steps, Lori advanced her spiritual growth. This is the difference between someone who merely adopts outer practices without a clear understanding of the spiritual path and someone like Lori who actually commits to her inner evolution. Although she started with just the practices, she eventually aligned her whole life with her new spiritual vision.

Spirituality is not a part-time pursuit that you can fit into your calendar like an activity or an appointment. It's not about doing a little meditation or some spiritual practices every now and then. Living as a spiritual being entails allowing a spiritual vision to color how you see, think, and respond to your *entire* life. All aspects of your personality—the physical, emotional, and intellectual—have to be involved and steadily developed so as to progress spiritually.[9] As the veiling, impurities, and restlessness in the mind are removed, the bliss of the Self slowly starts to shine through. With this process, there comes a deepening mental peace, poise, and happiness.

When we put in efforts to grow spiritually, we are described as being "on the path" or on a "spiritual journey." However, it isn't about physically going somewhere. It's an inner journey to uncover who we already are.

---

[9] Chinmayananda, *Penguin Swami Chinmayananda Reader,* 95.

CHAPTER 2

Spirituality and Religion

To assume differences in the world is to belie this great oneness in life.

> — *"Say Cheese!" Witty Wisdom*
> *by Swami Chinmayananda*

The Connection between Spirituality and Religion

Whenever we talk about spirituality, the topic of how it's different from religion invariably comes up. We can't seem to explain spirituality without referring to religion. What's the connection between spirituality and religion?

The term *spirit* refers to the spiritual essence or Supreme Cause that permeates all things and beings in creation. It is that which gives life to our personality and is our true Self. Spirituality is a knowledge or pursuit centered on the Self.[1] It doesn't refer to any *particular* activity but the *vision* with which we do

---

[1] Tejomayananda, *The Essence of Spirituality,* 11.

all our activities.[2] Practicing spirituality is looking beyond the differences in the world and holding a holistic view of oneness while interacting with it. All disciplines and practices aimed at living up to the vision of oneness and achieving oneness with spirit promote our spiritual growth.

Religion has two aspects—the outer rituals and practices, and the essential spiritual philosophy. Religion is generally misunderstood to be just the rituals and practices. If they are followed without an understanding of the underlying spiritual principles, religion declines into superstition. Conversely, if the spiritual fundamentals are learned without actually applying them in our lives, they remain dry theory. Both aspects have to go hand in hand, to bring out the true purpose and benefits of religion.[3] The rituals and practices are the actions to do, and the spiritual truths bring the right understanding and attitude behind the doing.

The Sanskrit term for religion is *matam*, which means "opinion".[4] Spiritual masters all over the world such as Jesus, Mohammad, Guru Nanak and Moses realized their oneness with spirit through their deep meditations and gained total fulfillment

---

[2] Ibid., 18.

[3] Chinmayananda, *Kena Upanishad*, 2.

[4] Chinmayananda, *Holy Geeta*, 204.

in life. With immense love and compassion for their fellow human beings, they selflessly shared their wisdom with them. The masters and their disciples interpreted and applied spiritual truths differently to suit the people of their time and the problems they faced.[5] They laid down teachings, practices, rituals and rules that became the basis of a religion.

To make the concept of spirit, the Supreme Cause easier for people to relate to, the enlightened masters personalized it and called it God and various other names such as *Lord, Holy Father, Allah, Elohim, Jehovah, Rama, Krishna, Vishnu* or *Ahura Mazda*. Whether God is referred to as He, She or It doesn't matter. The various names all point to the one supreme source of all that was, is and will ever be.[6]

Spirituality communicates the concept of God in a straightforward and factual way. For example, Vedanta defines it as, "...that from which these beings are born, that by which having been born, these beings live and continue to exist, and that unto which when departing, they all enter...[7] It uses abstract words to describe it such as *Self, Supreme Reality, Truth, the Absolute, the Life Principle, Om, Pure Awareness* and *Pure Consciousness*.[8]

---

[5] Ibid.

[6] Chinmayananda, *Penguin Swami Chinmayananda Reader*, 5.

[7] Chinmayananda, *Taittiriya Upanishad*, 3.1.2, 265.

[8] Chinmayananda, *Self-Unfoldment*, 34.

The spiritual masters brought God into the everyday lives of people. Here are two ways I conceive them doing this: Taking the spiritual truth that the Self is "all-pervading," the masters taught them that God is everywhere.[9] They reassured the people that God was always with them; loving, protecting, and guiding them throughout their lives. In difficult times, God's support would give them the strength to overcome loss and sorrow. From the truth, "The Self in all beings is One alone; residing in every being,"[10] the masters taught them that there is only one God and He dwells in the hearts of all people. Seeing the same benevolent God in all, people were advised to treat each other with love, kindness, respect, honesty and compassion.

Spirituality stands on its own while religions depend on spirituality. To illustrate the connection between spirituality and the various religions, I'll use something we can all easily relate to—food. If you were to cook a vegetable dish, you could use these basic ingredients: vegetables, salt, herbs, spices, water, and oil. Depending on your culture, tradition, and personal preferences, you would use the ingredients differently. For example, you could

---

[9] Chinmayananda, *Kaivalya Upanishad* 1.6, 30.
[10] Tejomayananda, *Amrtabindu Upanishad*, verse 12, 50.

make a Chinese stir-fry, an Indian curry or a French soup.

The food ingredients used for cooking represent spiritual principles, and religions are the many cuisines that use those ingredients to suit different people. How you use the ingredients doesn't really matter. What matters is that you end your hunger and gain a sense of contentment from eating the right quantity of nutritious and tasty food.

If we were to compare the practices of various religions, we would be focusing on the superficial differences. But, if we were to look at the fundamental teachings of the major world religions, we would find many similarities amongst them. Religions provide us with ways to end our worldly sorrows (represented by the hunger that we feel) and help us find the real happiness that we all seek (represented by the satisfaction of eating enough good food).

You may argue that you can simply eat the raw ingredients and survive just as well without cooking them. In other words, you could practice spirituality without religion. While this is true, the richness of the flavors and satisfaction of eating tasty food are brought out from cooking the raw ingredients and adding the condiments. Religions have "cooked" the ingredients—they have taken subtle spiritual principles which are difficult to grasp, explained them and made them readily applicable in our lives.

"I'm not Religious, I'm Spiritual"

Because of my interest in spirituality and passion for Vedanta, my conversations with people often flow in that direction. Time and again people make it a point to tell me, "I'm not religious, I'm *spiritual*." They are not agnostics or atheists but people who believe in a divine higher power that is the cause of the universe. They have chosen to connect with it in a personal way through their own practices.

There are various reasons why they have moved away from religion: One of the first things people tell me is that in some ways, religions seem to be stuck in time and haven't adequately supported changing societies and trends. Religious traditions and rules can be rigid and restrictive. They tell us how to dress, how often and in what way we should worship, what we should and shouldn't eat, and what to do on certain days of the week. In today's world, many of these religious rules and practices seem outdated and are difficult to follow. People openly admit that they neither relate to them, nor do they see a need for religious institutions, leaders or dogma. They seldom or never go to a place of worship such as a temple, church or mosque to pray.

Some people tell me that the many prescribed daily religious rituals can become mechanical and feel more like chores than inspiration. They complain that when they have questioned the reasoning behind the rituals, they are not always answered and when they are, the responses are inadequate as they don't satisfy their logical mind. People questioned less in the past, but today's seekers are more discerning and demand convincing answers.

When religious practices are not understood, explained incorrectly, or simply inconvenient, we tend to let them go. I can personally relate to this because as I was growing up, my mother would complain of my incessant questioning about the many Hindu observances that she followed. She couldn't give me satisfactory answers and didn't understand why I wouldn't simply follow what I was told. "I never asked any questions of *my* mother," she would say in exasperation. Not surprisingly, I dropped many of the observances simply because I didn't understand why they were meaningful or important.

Considering these facts, you may be thinking that spirituality is the way to go. There certainly are advantages to practicing spirituality: You are not tied to any dogma, specific rules or practices. It encourages independent thinking in trying to understand life, universal laws, the world, and its source. You have the freedom to practice it in any way that evokes genuine feelings in you. It moderates behavior through the knowledge of the essential unity of all life. This creates a sense of connection and harmony with other people, animals, nature and the earth. You chart out your own moral compass and act on beliefs that you have faith in and that feel true to you.

Although these facts are true, it's important to remember that while spirituality gives us the vision of life, it doesn't elaborate on how to live it. It tells us the goal (the Self) but doesn't provide details on how to achieve it. As explained earlier, spirituality needs application. If we are going to design our own means and practices, why not take those that are already tried and tested by religion? Why not practice spirituality within the parameters of religion?

Practicing Your Own Blend of Spirituality and Religion

Humanity has turned to religion for peace and solace for many centuries. When life's challenges cannot be resolved through worldly means, we often look to religion for answers. It fills a void in our lives that can only be gratified with faith and love for the divine higher power. It provides a well-established, structured system of living, following which we are promised peace of mind and ultimate happiness.

Religion helps to transform our lives by teaching us how to master ourselves. It builds up our resilience so that we can face challenging circumstances with a peaceful mind and be happy in spite of them.[11] It shows us ways to connect with and cultivate love for God. The soulful prayers and devotional hymns uplift our minds and fill our hearts. The various disciplines, austerities and practices build integrity of character and mastery over the mind. The do's and don'ts help people to stay on the path of moral living so that they don't suffer the sorrowful consequences of wrong actions.

Spirituality and religion are not mutually exclusive. A spiritual person may also be religious, and a religious person may be spiritual. We can live spiritual truths within the framework of the religion that we practice. Mahatma Gandhi and Mother Teresa are two well-known people who did this.

Mahatma Gandhi was a devout Hindu who found strength, courage, and wisdom in the teachings of the holy book called the *Bhagavad Gita*. He fought to

---

[11] Chinmayananda, *Self-Unfoldment,* 30.

gain India's independence from British rule, while holding fast to the spiritual ideal of nonviolence. He understood that we are all one and there is no need to harm others even as we stand firm on our goals and principles. He said," My religion is based on truth and nonviolence. Truth is my God. Nonviolence is the means of realizing Him."

Mother Teresa was a Catholic nun and missionary with a spiritual vision. "I heard the call to give up all and follow Christ into the slums to serve Him among the poorest of the poor," she said. Her vision was spiritual (unity with others and, therefore, love and serve all unconditionally), and her love for Christ came from her religious background. So, being religious and spiritual can and do go hand in hand.

Religions provide guidance for living a happy life. If you are not finding this in your religion, you may want to look beyond the outer practices, rituals and dogma and seek out the beauty of the spiritual teachings that lie within. The problems in religion arise from their interpretation and application. These are secondary to the underlying spiritual principles that they stand on.

If your elders or the leaders of your faith are not able to answer your questions about your religion, you may consider doing a little research on your own. There's always a supporting spiritual philosophy and science behind the teachings. When you discover the purpose, and even the cultural and historical backdrop of the teachings and practices, you may be able to better appreciate the reasoning behind them. This is what I am learning to do.

Maybe going to a place of worship to pray with others doesn't appeal to you. You may prefer to connect with the divine on your own, once a day or more. Perhaps you might think about doing both—occasionally joining in some congregational services, as well as practicing your own spiritual discipline daily. Religious gatherings can be very uplifting. There is a totally different energy when many people pray together, when compared to individually. However, it's also not enough to only participate in religious services. You must keep up the inspiration and your efforts to grow on your own by applying what you learn in your daily life. It may be a good idea to have one foundational faith that you can grow in. If you adopt the practices and teachings from various faiths, you may find it hard to form one definite and meaningful connection to the supreme Self.

Just as faith in God is an integral part of religion, faith in the Supreme Reality is essential in spirituality. All practices, whether religious or spiritual are directed towards expressions of that power. If your religious rituals and practices are becoming dry and mechanical, you can add a little spirituality to your religion. In other words, you can do them consciously with understanding and an attitude of love. This will increase your focus and commitment to them. Putting your heart into what you are doing is important whether you consider yourself religious or spiritual.

People who say that they are not religious but are spiritual, and then do nothing about it, are neither religious nor spiritual. In fact, they think that merely *saying* they are spiritual gives them permission to discard religion and be free to live as they want.

Even though I don't follow many of the Hindu observances, I'm not focused on rituals, and I don't go to a temple regularly, I honestly cannot do without my religious faith. The biggest gift that my mother gave me is my faith in God. I look to my faith for the teachings that help me deal with daily problems and to connect to the Self. I have a dedicated space for prayer, reflection and meditation which I use daily. I have set up an altar where I have placed symbols of the divine to uplift my mind. Here is where I read and study my books on Vedanta, write my reflections in a journal, chant Sanskrit verses and Hindu prayers, use my *mala* (rosary) to repeat *mantras* (sacred chants), and perform a couple of special prayer rituals every now and then. I have taken up the practices and discipline that I understand and feel most connected to.

Since I am Hindu, I'd like to explain something that baffles many people about Hinduism. It is believed that Hindus worship many Gods, but this is not true. We understand that God is infinite and can thus manifest in a countless number of ways. Since it is not possible to conceive an infinite, formless God, Hindus worship Him/Her/It in the form of symbols or idols. The idols are not worshiped *as* God, but they are symbols that *represent* God. We worship the *ideals* represented in those idols.[12]

As a spiritual being on the path of inner growth, it's important that you stay open and respectful of the teachings and practices of all faiths. They lead to the same goal—God or the *Truth*. Each religion provides solutions to meeting life's challenges and ways of worshipping God in its own unique way. Holding on to the spiritual truth of being one with all, you may find great value in practicing the religion you were born into or choose to adopt. When you commit to your spiritual growth and consistently work towards it, you will bring out the beauty of the spiritual Self within you. A harmonious blend of spirituality and religion can take you to that goal.

---

[12] Chinmayananda, *Penguin Swami Chinmayananda Reader*, 7.

CHAPTER 3

The Rare Gift of Being Born as a Human

Among all living creatures, a human birth is indeed rare.

—Adi Shankaracharya, *Vivekachoodamani*

Just How Rare Is a Human Birth?

If someone gave you a beautiful diamond ring, you would happily thank the giver of the ring. But would you remember to be thankful for the finger on which you're able to wear the ring in the first place? Have you stopped to think about the greatest gift that you have—the gift of a human life?[1]

Have you ever wondered why you are a human being and not one of the other millions of species of life on the planet? Why are you not an animal or bird, fish, or even an insect? Human life is sacred

---

[1] Tejomayananda et al., "Life Is a Gift, Living Is an Art," 6.

and precious; Vedanta tells us that gaining a human body is very, very rare.

Now, you might be thinking we can't be *that* rare if there are over seven billion of us on the planet. That's what I thought too, until I visited the Royal Ontario Museum in downtown Toronto, with my son's grade 6 class many years ago. There I came across a display called "The Wheel of Life." It was a large, colorful wheel that could be spun around, much like the wheel in the American television game show *Wheel of Fortune*. It was sectioned into pie-like segments and had many wooden pegs attached at regular intervals along the periphery. A flexible pointer was mounted on the outside of the wheel. Its pointed edge reached a few inches into the wheel. Visitors could hold on to one of the pegs and spin the wheel. As the wheel turned, the pointer flapped against the pegs until it came to rest between two pegs on one of the wheel's segments.

The segments represented the various categories of species found on Earth. They were listed by their difficult-to-pronounce, scientific Latin names. Very roughly, here's what I understood: Insects made up the largest segment on the wheel, about half; plants made up about one quarter; fungi, mold, algae, protozoa, and other simple organisms made up about one eighth; and vertebrates and invertebrates represented the last one eighth.

There was an intriguing question at the top of the wheel: *If you were born into a species entirely by chance, what chance would you have of being born a human?*

Visitors were asked to spin the wheel and see which segment they would land on. It was a fun game of chance to see which species you would likely be born into. I noticed that the children were enjoying spinning the wheel and teasing each other. The wheel repeatedly landed on either the segment of insects or plants, and the children were having fun calling each other bugs and beetles. Smiling to myself, I thought, "If my birth were determined as randomly as a spin on this wheel, I would've had a far greater chance of being born an insect or a weed than a human being!"

I wondered how I could spin the wheel so that it would land on the segment representing human beings. I went closer and carefully looked all around the wheel for *Homo sapiens,* the scientific term for the human species. But I couldn't find it. Next to it was a display that explained why: Humans make up such a tiny sliver of the total number of species that we could not be represented on this wheel!

This is not surprising, since humans are *only one* of all the species of life on land and in the oceans.

When compared to the myriads of possible species that we could have been born into, the fact that we are now humans *is* remarkable. Even from the standpoint of sheer numbers, we are rare. Seven or eight billion humans is an insignificant number when compared to the uncountable other living beings. It is not by luck or a random act of nature that we are now human beings. It is a privilege that is gained from the merits of many previous lifetimes.[2] The spiritual masters of Vedanta tell us to wake up to this fact and find out more about our special purpose as human beings so that we can make the best use of our lives.

Our Human Gifts

We have lived countless past lives in other species before evolving into human beings.[3] We are the highest and most evolved of all the species. Gurudev, Swami Chinmayananda, vouches for this fact when he says, "Man is the roof and crown of creation."[4] Nature has nothing more to do to improve our bodies. The next step in our evolution lies in our *own* efforts to develop our intellectual and psychological

---

2 Tejomayananda, *Living Vedanta,* 18–19.

3 Chinmayananda, *Vivekachoodamani,* 9–10.

4 Chinmayananda, *Kindle Life, 46.*

personalities.[5] What gives us this capability and sets us apart from the other species in the animal kingdom is our highly developed intellect.

The Sanskrit word for "animal" is *pashu*, which means the one who "sees" things only superficially.[6] Animals take what they see at face value, as they don't have a capacity to think deeply about things. They function mainly by instinct. For example, if a squirrel finds an acorn on the ground, it doesn't question where it came from, how long it's been lying there, or what are its nutritional benefits. It simply sees it as something edible. The Sanskrit word for "human," *manushya*, is noteworthy. It is derived from the root *man*, which means "to think."[7] Thinking is our special ability.

Thinking allows us to learn new knowledge and skills to improve our lives and how we respond to it. Our sophisticated intellect can think logically, conceptually, laterally, abstractly, creatively, imaginatively, critically, and in numerous other ways. It has enabled us to develop various sciences, whole cities, a multitude of inventions for our daily living, and technological marvels like computers and the internet.

---

[5] Chinmayananda, *Vivekachoodamani*, 10.
[6] Tejomayananda, *Hindu Culture*, 21.
[7] Ibid.

But aside from achieving these great outer accomplishments, the human intellect has some other unique inner competencies that distinguish it from the other species. The lives of animals are programmed by nature. They cannot willfully change their deep-seated tendencies and behavior. For example, a tiger cannot choose to become vegetarian, and bees cannot make better beehives. We, however, can change our behavior and habits.

We can use our intellect's capacity for discernment to turn the focus of our attention inward and be aware of what we are thinking and doing at any given moment. Based on this information, our intellect can then guide us to substitute undesirable or negative thoughts and actions with positive or loving ones. Visualizing our desired outcomes, we can amplify our willpower and enthusiasm toward gaining our goals. By consistently taking the right actions in the right direction, we can gradually introduce the new habits into our lives.

We can feel and express noble emotions and virtues such as devotion, contentment, compassion, forgiveness, straightforwardness, calmness, humility, patience, and self-control. Our intellect can help us sublimate lower emotions and impulses and develop noble qualities in greater measure. For example, we can cultivate acceptance or patience by thinking about the fact that expressing anger or impatience doesn't change a situation or a person. It merely aggravates our own mind and often hurts the other person's feelings. If we repeatedly align our actions with the virtues we are trying to adopt, we can gradually incorporate them into our own personality.

The human intellect has the subtlety to ponder deep philosophical, moral, and ethical matters. Naturally then, spirituality and religion are only for humans. Animals don't contemplate life or question the existence of a creator. We question where we came from, where we go after death, what our purpose is, and how to achieve it. We inquire into the nature of the universe, the source, and where to find it. We are able to cultivate our faith and worship God in any form that appeals to us. Seeking and finding the answers to existential questions and engaging in devotional practices helps us to grow spiritually.

What brings our greatest spiritual growth is meditation. Only we can meditate. Gurudev called it "the highest vocation of man."[8] Using our intellect to guide our thoughts, we can intentionally quiet them and enjoy inner peace of mind, without depending on outer things, people, or circumstances.[9] No

---

[8] Chinmayananda, *Art of Man-Making*, 292.

[9] Chinmayananda, *Self-Unfoldment*, 13.

matter how intelligent an ape, elephant, or dolphin, it cannot quiet its thoughts to meditate. Even if you worry that you can't quiet your thoughts, just remember that it's a skill you *can* learn. Animals don't even know they have minds, let alone that they may wish to quiet them.

Our special human gifts stem from a well-developed intellect. Using it intelligently, we have brought about vast improvements in our outer environment and daily living. The greatest gift, however, is being able to use it to advance our personal and spiritual growth. "No other sentient being in the universe has the equipment for thus hastening its own evolution as efficiently as we can."[10]

Using Our Gifts

To strive for the Truth is the highest of all conscious efforts of a human being.
—Swami Chinmayananda, *Meditation and Life*

As explained in chapter 1, because we don't recognize our true spiritual nature, we wrongly identify with our finite human personalities. This then gives rise to a sense of incompleteness and

---

[10] Chinmayananda, *Meditation and Life,* 32.

many desires to fulfill ourselves.[11] When we drop our erroneous identification, our true spiritual nature will be clearly known to us. We won't need to produce it or get it from somewhere else.[12] In fact, it's already present right here and now, but simply not recognized by us. This fact can be illustrated by a simple example:

Take a glass of clean, pure water and a teaspoon of dirt. The water represents spirit, and the dirt represents our false identification. When we add the dirt to the water and stir it up, the water will appear dirty. But note that the water hasn't intrinsically changed. When we filter and distill it, we will regain the clean, pure water that was always there. It was simply not recognized as such because we were looking at the contaminants that were suspended in it. In the same way, spirit, our true essence, is right here, but not recognized by us because of our identification with our human personality.

Our spiritual essence is the great truth that we have to rediscover. It is our ultimate goal. When we realize it, we will find permanent happiness and fulfill the ultimate purpose of our human lives.[13] How do we do it? A human being has a physical body,

---

[11] Refer to the section "Being on the Path" in chapter 1.

[12] Chinmayananda, *Self-Unfoldment*, 41.

[13] Chinmayananda, *Meditation and Life*, 36.

emotions, and an intellect.[14] These three aspects have to be used in special ways to break down the ego, which arises out of our false identification.

At the body level, the spiritual masters recommend that we work selflessly for others, lovingly dedicating our actions to a noble cause or God.[15] Volunteer work in the community, at a place of worship, or in a social service organization provides us opportunities to do actions in this way. However, we don't need to go out looking for special work. Even our everyday duties can help erode the ego if we do them with a selfless attitude.

Emotionally, we can dilute the ego by cultivating a loving heart. We can do this by being kind, helpful, caring, giving, and loving of others. We should be mindful that we do this with a genuine and heartfelt feeling, and without ulterior motives.

Our intellect is to be engaged in seeking out what causes sorrow in life, how to end it, and where true happiness lies. In his book the *Vivekachoodamani*, the great Vedantic master Adi Shankaracharya (788 AD – 820 AD) explains the root cause of sorrow. He tells us that ignorance of our spiritual identity, and the consequent identification with our human aspects—what he calls the "not-Self"—is "bondage"

---

[14] Chinmayananda, *Self-Unfoldment*, 32.
[15] Tejomayananda, *Living Vedanta*, 20.

and therefore brings suffering.[16] In verse 49 he describes how a sincere spiritual seeker with an urgency to put an end to his or her worldly sorrows approaches a master and pleads for an answer to his or her burning questions:

> What is bondage? How has it come? How does it continue to exist? How can one get out of it completely? What is the not-Self? Who is the supreme Self? And what is the process of discrimination between these two (Self and not-Self)? Please explain all these to me.[17]

Gaining the answers to such profound questions from a spiritual master brings clarity and peace in the mind of the seeker. Then, following the teacher's guidance, he or she gradually learns to destroy the ego by rediscovering the Self within during meditation.

Why meditation? Vedanta explains that the final goal of life, the realization of our spiritual essence, is to be gained in meditation.[18] Having gained a full understanding of the nature of the Self and not-Self, it is in meditation that we can make use of the intellect's capacity for subtle discernment to detach from our

---

false identification and come to "rediscover ourselves to be in essence nothing but the eternally sweet spirit."[19]

Gurudev tells us that we will not have any interest or enthusiasm to walk the spiritual path unless we understand the sanctity and the preciousness of our human life.[20] Once we do, we will realize that nature has given us a very rare chance to achieve the highest bliss, and ultimate fulfillment in life. Gaining this vital understanding will give us the inspiration and motivation to make the best use of our unique human abilities to promote our inner development, and eventually rediscover the perfection of our true Self. When we attain it, we will reach the acme of our evolution.[21]

This is the rare gift of being born as a human.

---

[19] Chinmayananda, *Meditation and Life*, 23.

[20] Chinmayananda, *Talks on Sankara's Vivekachudamani*, DVD, lecture 1.

[21] Chinmayananda, *Kindle Life*, 105.

CHAPTER 4

Proof That You Are a Spiritual Being

The popular misconception is that man is a body with a soul. However, the truth is that man is the soul in a body; he is eternal.

—Swami Chinmayananda,
The Penguin Swami Chinmayananda Reader

What Is Spirit?

Every single thing and being has both an apparent identity and an essential nature. The apparent identity of an object or being constitutes its outer characteristics, while its essential nature is the fundamental substance from which it is made. For example, take a clay jug: The shape, form, and color of the jug make up its apparent identity; clay is its essential nature. The apparent identity depends on the fundamental substance for its existence. Without clay, a clay jug would not exist.

The apparent identity keeps changing and dies

away, but the essential nature is unchanging. Think about how the jug will start to fade in color and fall apart over time. Or consider that you can take a hammer to the jug and break it. But no matter what happens to the jug, the clay will always remain clay. It was there before the jug was formed, it exists in the form of the jug now, and it will remain after the jug is destroyed.[1]

Human beings are no different. Each of us has both an apparent identity and an essential nature. Our apparent identity arises out of our identification with our changing bodies, emotions, and thoughts. It's easy to see how these are constantly changing: Our bodies look and function differently as we go through the various stages of our lives—infancy, childhood, adolescence, young adulthood, middle age, and old age. Our bodies change when our health changes, when we are physically injured, or when we gain or lose weight. Our emotions vary throughout the day. A cheerful mood can quickly turn into anger, sadness, or frustration if we hear unkind words, watch a disturbing news story, or experience a challenge. And finally, our thoughts change so quickly that it's impossible to predict what thought will arise in the very next moment.

When I identify with the fluctuating conditions

---

[1] Chinmayananda, *Self-Unfoldment,* 35.

of my body, emotions, and thoughts, my apparent identity also changes. For example, identifying with my body, I might say, "I was able to fit into these jeans five years ago but not now." Or, identifying with my emotions, I might say, "I was anxious when I arrived late to the airport, but I was relieved to find out that my flight was delayed by fifty minutes." Or, identifying with my thoughts, I might say, "I used to be a conservative, but now my political values are more in alignment with the liberal party."

Our essential nature, on the other hand, is something distinctly different. It is spirit that remains unchanged in the past, in the present, and in the future.[2] Spirit enables you to recognize the changes that occur in your apparent identity.[3] These changes do not affect your essential nature. As with the example of the clay, spirit is present before you are born, it remains while you are alive, and it continues to exist even after you die. Without spirit, you could not exist.

It's easy to understand that a clay jug cannot exist without clay. It's harder to accept that without spirit we would not exist. To look at spirit, we must first examine matter, which has qualities that are the opposite of spirit.

---

[2] Ibid., 34.
[3] Ibid.

48

Your apparent identity is made up of physical and nonphysical matter. Vedanta uses the terms *gross* and *subtle* matter.[4] The physical body is gross matter. It is perceived by the five sense organs—eyes, ears, nose, tongue, and skin. The emotions and thoughts are subtle matter, that is, beyond the perception of the sense organs. You can't see, hear, smell, taste, or touch emotions or thoughts. Matter, whether gross or subtle, is intrinsically inert and lacks sentience.[5] In other words, it is neither alive nor conscious. It doesn't move or function on its own, and it can't perceive, feel, or know things.

Now, if your body, emotions, and thoughts are merely matter, how is it that you're able to perceive, feel, and know? Vedanta points out that spirit is Pure Consciousness that expresses as life when it comes into contact with matter.[6] To explain this idea, spirit can be compared to electricity and a light bulb to matter. A light bulb doesn't give off light on its own. But when electricity comes into contact with it, it glows.[7] Similarly, in the presence of spirit, the gross and subtle matter aspects of a human being appear alive and conscious.

To illustrate how spirit animates matter, imagine

[4] Ibid., 135, 136.
[5] Ibid., 32.
[6] Ibid., 32, 33.
[7] Ibid., 33.

that you're out shopping with a friend for a Halloween costume. You walk into a store displaying a variety of costumes, all of them hanging limp and lifeless on racks. Even the costume of the great physicist Albert Einstein, complete with a full head mask, can neither move nor speak. You try it on.

The costume represents matter and you represent spirit. You insert your right foot into one floppy pant leg, which straightens as your leg goes in. You then push your left foot into the other pant leg and pull the suit up to your waist. Next, you insert your arms into the droopy sleeves and zip up the costume. What was once a flat costume has become animated, taking on the distinct shape of your body. Finally, you put on the head mask and walk over to the mirror. Spirit has completely pervaded matter—and Einstein has come to life! The costume can now move, walk, and talk. Your friend taps you on the shoulder and says jokingly, "Hi, Einstein!" You turn around, wave your hand cheerily, and respond, "Hi!"

Like the costume, the body and mind are incapable of acting, feeling, or thinking. But when they're enlivened by spirit, body and mind appear to be alive and functioning.

Why We Cannot See Spirit

If we are spirit, you might ask, why can't we see it with our eyes or understand it with our minds?

As inert matter, the eyes and mind have no sentience with which to understand spirit. Both the seeing capacity of the eyes and the thinking ability of the mind come from spirit itself. So they can't see or know spirit.[8]

To illustrate this point, let's use an example of a TV. For fun, let's pretend it can think and talk. One day, in a contemplative mood, Ms. TV decides that she wants to experience the cause of her own thinking and talking abilities (electricity) outside herself. She searches for the source of that electricity and finds that it's coming from the wall outlet. In an attempt to see electricity, she pulls out the plug. What happens? Ms. TV immediately dies! She can't see or experience the presence of what enlivens her *outside herself*. It's only *because* of electricity that Ms. TV can function. In the same way, we can neither use our eyes to see nor use our minds to know spirit outside ourselves. We are alive and functioning because of the presence of spirit.

The other reason we can't see spirit is that being consciousness, spirit is the inner subject that knows

---

[8] Ibid., 141.

all objects. And so, it can't be known or thought of as an object.[9] We can only infer the presence of spirit, and we do so by looking at its expressions.

Let's use another example of electricity. You know that electricity is present when a toaster toasts bread, a fan circulates air, and a microwave oven cooks food. These are all expressions of electricity. A functioning TV, as in the previous example, is also an expression of electricity. You can't see electricity directly, but you can infer its presence by looking at its expressions. In the same way, you can infer that spirit is present in you because you're able to read and understand this book. A conscious living being, functioning and interacting with the world, is an expression of spirit. Without the enlivening presence of spirit, you would die. When you say that you are a spiritual being, it means that you are spirit expressing itself through a human body.

Although I've used electricity as an example to explain spirit, I'd like to clarify that electricity is energy, but spirit is *not* energy. Energy belongs to the realm of matter. Spirit is consciousness and beyond matter. It gives life and energy to matter.

---

[9] Tejomayananda, *Amrtabindu Upanishad,* verse 6, 26.

Our Vital Organs Do Not Keep Us Alive

Even though you may have understood what spirit is, you may not be fully convinced that we are spiritual beings. Can we *prove* it?

Science tells us that when our vital organs, such as the brain or heart, stop functioning, we stop functioning and die. And we know that people with failing organs who receive healthy organ transplants continue to live. Therefore it seems logical that our organs are what keep us alive. Is this true? Let's think about it—what makes organs, such as the brain or heart, function?

One Saturday morning, I switched channels on my TV, looking for something interesting to watch. I came across a fund-raising drive organized by a hospital here in Toronto, Canada. The hospital was highlighting the great work that it was doing by showing stories of children whom its doctors had helped. I watched the story of a baby born with a congenital heart defect who needed a new heart to survive. The hospital found a suitable heart from a baby in a neighboring city who had died soon after birth. Thankfully, the parents of that baby had consented to donate their baby's heart to give another child the gift of life.

The doctors rushed the healthy heart by

helicopter to the hospital in Toronto where the recipient baby was waiting. I saw the doctor hurry down the corridor to the operating theater, carrying the heart in an insulated cooler lined with ice. Inside the operating theater, the baby had been prepared and was ready for her new heart. Luckily, the heart transplant was successful, and the baby received a new lease on life.

Let's think about a couple of possible situations. Let's say that the heart came too late, and the recipient baby died while waiting. Would the donated heart have the ability to bring the dead baby back to life? Or what if the cells of the living heart had died in transit? Would the dead organ be of any use to the living baby? Of course, the answer to both scenarios is no. A successful outcome would occur only if a *living* donor organ was speedily transplanted into an *already living* body.

It's clear from these scenarios that the organs don't keep the body alive. If that were true, you would be a mere assembly of various parts functioning together. Any time a part grew old or malfunctioned, you would replace that part with a healthy one and be alive and whole again. Using the same logic, a person with an amputated arm or leg would be "less" of a person than he or she was previously. We know that this is not the case. What happens to your body parts does not affect the real you. This is because you are spirit, the vital and conscious presence that keeps your body alive and makes it function.

Not convinced? Let's go deeper and talk about death . . .

Only the Body Dies

Vedanta asserts that the essential nature of a thing holds up, or supports, the existence of the thing.[10] Without its essence, a thing would cease to be. For instance, fire gives off light and heat; they are its essential nature. There can be no fire if they are absent. So if something looks like fire but isn't hot, you know that it's not fire. Candles or tea lights that are battery operated mimic fire by emitting light, but they give off no heat. In the same way, according to Vedanta, without the presence of spirit in a human being, there wouldn't *be* a human being. The body would be merely inert matter.

Is this true? Does spirit support our existence because it's our essential nature?

Have you ever been to a funeral, looked at the dead body, and wondered what had happened to the person who was once there? It's hard to believe that

---

[10] Chinmayananda, *Self-Unfoldment,* 223.

he or she no longer exists. The body is there, but the real person has disappeared without a trace.

I used to teach spiritual fundamentals to teenagers. I asked one class if anyone had experienced a death in the family or had seen a dead body. One of the students answered that she had recently gone through such an experience. She said, "We were with Grandma when she was in the hospital, and we were there when they came to take the body away." I pointed out that she had said they were with "Grandma" when she was alive and then naturally called what her grandmother had left behind after death as "the body." Why had she done that? She herself was surprised and didn't know why. I asked her if she had ever thought that the body was still Grandma. Visibly taken aback by the suggestion that she would ever confuse the dead body for her grandmother, she answered without hesitation "No!" There was no doubt in her mind that the dead body was not her grandmother. Her grandmother was gone.

Intuitively, we know that we're not our bodies. Think about how we describe a person who has died. Don't we say "She's *passed* away" or "She's dead and *gone*"?[11] Life in the body is sustained by the life-giving factor called spirit. This is our essential

---

[11] Chinmayananda, *Holy Bhagavad Gita,* DVD, chapter 2.

nature, which holds up, or supports, the existence of our apparent identity. This is why when we leave our bodies, they die.

Death is only for the physical body. We are eternal spiritual beings, separate and different from our perishable bodies.

Spirit, the Silent Inner Witness

There is yet another way to prove that we are spiritual beings. Vedanta explains that we experience three states of consciousness every day—the waking state, the dream state, and the deep sleep state.[12]

In the waking state, you identify with your physical body and are aware of the waking world. In the dream state, your consciousness moves to a dream world of experiences created by your mind. And in the deep sleep state, you know no objects, emotions, or thoughts. You experience nothing but an undisturbed deep sleep. When you wake up, you say that you slept well. You take on different identities as you move through these three states: the waker, the dreamer, and the deep sleeper.[13]

Consider this: The waker, the dreamer, and the deep sleeper are three separate identities existing

---

[12] Tejomayananda, *Tattvabodha,* 55.

[13] Chinmayananda, *Self-Unfoldment,* 138.

in three different planes of consciousness. Each one negates the others, so how are we able to remember our experiences in all three states?

This is possible only because there's a separate, unchanging entity within us who witnesses our experiences in the three states and is unaffected by them all. It's like when you, an individual, take on different roles in your everyday life. So whether you're being a parent to your child, a passenger on a bus, or a customer at a store, the real "you" doesn't change. At the end of the day, you remember all the roles that you played because you were present and witnessed them all. Your true Self is spirit, and spirit is "the witness of the three states of consciousness."[14]

Here's a simpler way to demonstrate the presence of this inner witness. Take a few quiet minutes for this reflection.

In your mind's eye, picture yourself in the various stages of your life: preschooler, child, teenager, and adult. See every decade of your life up till now. Try to remember what you looked like. Note what experiences stand out in your mind. As you look back, notice that there's an "I" that has remained unchanged through the countless inner and outer experiences of your life. This "I" is present right now

---

[14] Tejomayananda, *Tattvabodha*, 35.

as you read this page. This is the real you. You are spirit, the silent witness of them all.

I realize that the ideas I have shared with you in this chapter require some personal reflection. You'll have to turn them over and over in your mind, and ask yourself, "Is this true? Does this make sense?" Time spent in quiet contemplation is vital for every spiritual seeker. This will allow the new ideas to sink in and become your own.

I once made a cup of coffee for a friend and added sugar. When she tasted it, she winced and pushed the coffee away. "It's bitter!" she said. I answered, "I have added two teaspoons of sugar to your coffee. Stir it and see!" Spiritual concepts are like that—it's only when you stir them over within yourself that they can sweeten your life.

CHAPTER 5

Your True Nature

You are not the body; you are the essence, the Self (Atman), the divine entity within.
—Swami Chinmayananda,
Meditation and Life

Spirit Concealed in Matter

Spirit is hiding in plain sight. It's right here, yet we don't recognize it. Why is this so? Think of a nugget of pure gold. If the gold is heated, melted, and shaped into a necklace, we don't call it "gold" anymore. Looking at its appearance, we call it "a necklace." The name and form of the necklace "hide" the fundamental substance that gives the necklace its existence—gold. This is the same reason we see and experience only our human bodies and personalities. Even though spirit is our true essence, it appears to be hidden behind these material coverings. We have forgotten that we are pure spirit, just as we forget that the necklace is nothing but gold.

If you were "It" in a game of hide-and-seek, you would begin by searching and eliminating all the places where the "hider" could be until you eventually find him. Similarly, to reclaim spirit, you can begin by first learning about the matter aspects of your personality and then rejecting them as your true Self. In this chapter, I explain these matter aspects and the nature of spirit. I do this through a chart created by Swami Chinmayananda.

Gurudev was a consummate teacher who conveyed deep spiritual ideas with exceptional clarity. This concise chart of only ten letters and one symbol encapsulates the answers to some fundamental questions such as:

1. What is the Ultimate Cause of creation and where can it be found?
2. What is our essential nature?
3. What prevents us from recognizing our own divinity?
4. What is the ego, and where does it come from?
5. What factors constitute the world of our experiences?

It is known simply as "Swami Chinmayananda's Body-Mind-Intellect Chart."[1]

Swami Chinmayananda's Body-Mind-Intellect Chart

The symbol at the top is the Sanskrit word *Om*. *Om* represents spirit, or the Self. The other ten letters represent various aspects of the world of matter. For now, I'll skip over the explanation of *Om* and the letter *V*, and begin with the other nine letters.

The letters *B, M,* and *I* represent the *Body*, the *Mind*, and the *Intellect*. These are the *tools* with which we function in, and transact with, the world.

The Body. Our physical body was formed from the essence of the food eaten by our parents; it is sustained by the food that we eat every day and becomes food for other living organisms after its death.[2] It houses the five organs of perception—eyes, ears, nose, tongue, and skin. With the eyes, we see form and color; the ears hear sounds; the nose takes in smells; the tongue tastes; and the skin gives us the sense of touch.

The letters *M* and *I* represent two types of

---

[1] You can listen to an explanation of the chart by Swami Chinmayananda himself in *The Logic of Spirituality: An Introduction to Vedanta*, DVD.

[2] Chinmayananda, *Self-Unfoldment*, 125.

thoughts. Vedanta differentiates them based on their function. Feeling thoughts are called the "mind," and thinking thoughts are called the "intellect."

The Mind. The mind is the seat of our emotions.[3] Why are emotions considered thoughts? Although it's true that we feel emotions within the body, they first arise in the mind as thoughts. For example, you receive an e-mail from a dear friend in another country. In it is the good news that she's expecting her first baby. But unless you open her e-mail and read it, you won't experience any happy feelings. Only when your mind comes into contact with her words will you feel happy.

The Intellect. The intellect is the seat of reason and judgment. This is where thinking, judging, analyzing, and decision making reside. I like to compare it to the voice of the global positioning system (GPS) in my car. It provides clear, rational guidance on where to go next. When I change my mind and decide to go somewhere else, it never gets angry, annoyed, or irritated. It continues to repeat its original instructions in a calm, clear way. Of course, as humans, we think *and* feel, so thankfully, we will never become as unfeeling as a GPS!

Skipping over to the third row, the letters *O, E,* and *T* represent *Objects, Emotions,* and *Thoughts.*

---

[3] Ibid., 128.

63

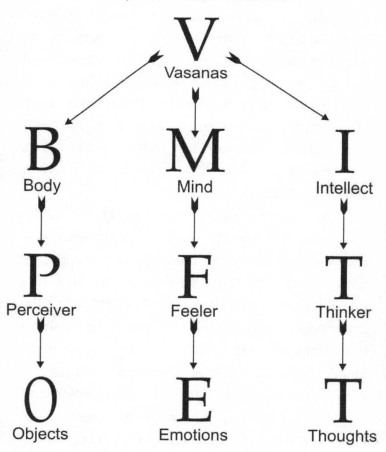

Supreme ConsciousnessSupreme Consciousness

Vasanas

B — Body
M — Mind
I — Intellect

P — Perceiver
F — Feeler
T — Thinker

O — Objects
E — Emotions
T — Thoughts

©Central Chinmaya Mission Trust©Central Chinmaya Mission Trust

Objects, Emotions, and Thoughts. With the five sense organs of the body, we experience the world of objects comprising forms and colors, sounds, smells, tastes, and textures. With the mind, we experience the world of emotions such as joy, anger, jealousy, love, and fear. With the intellect, we experience the world of thoughts (ideas). Objects, emotions, and thoughts make up the *fields of our experience.*[4]

Now, let's make the connection between the tools of experience (the first row of letters) and the fields of experiences (the third row of letters). The letters *P, F,* and *T* in the second row stand for the *Perceiver, Feeler,* and *Thinker.*

Perceiver, Feeler, and Thinker. Starting from left to right, look down in the direction of the arrows in the chart to understand the following: Identifying with the body, the experiencer becomes the perceiver, perceiving the world of objects. When the experiencer identifies with the mind, he or she is the feeler who feels emotions. And the experiencer identifying with the intellect becomes the thinker who thinks thoughts.[5] The perceiver, feeler, and thinker identities together are the experiencer, also known as the "ego."[6] The ego does not refer to an

---

[4] Ibid., 31.

[5] Ibid., 31–32.

[6] Ibid., 41.

inflated sense of self as it is commonly understood. The ego in Vedanta is the notion of individuality that arises when the experiencer identifies with the body, mind, and intellect and their characteristics.[7]

In short, the ego (you and I), functioning as a *Perceiver-Feeler-Thinker,* uses the tools of the *Body-Mind-Intellect* to transact and gather its experiences from the world comprising of *Objects-Emotions-Thoughts.*

The Soul

To consider yourself as a separate individual, a Mr. Smith or Mrs. Jones, is as foolish as for each billowing wave to consider itself separate from the ocean.
—Swami Chinmayananda, *Meditation and Life*

Vedanta explains that spirit and soul are essentially the same. From the larger perspective of the world, spirit expresses as life in all beings. That's why it's described as *Supreme Consciousness* in the chart. However, when spirit enlivens a *particular* being, it's known as the individual soul. We are individual souls whose real nature is spirit, which is why we are called spiritual beings. Here's a simple way to think of it: If spirit is compared to the ocean, the soul would be an individual wave. A wave is the ocean expressing in that form.

---

[7] Tejomayananda, *Living Vedanta,* 62.

We can take this analogy and connect it with the chart. The wave—the soul, not recognizing its essential blissful and limitless nature—erroneously identifies with its limited size, shape, and characteristics (body, mind, and intellect). It starts thinking of itself as an individual wave (perceiver, feeler, and thinker). If it's a big wave, it feels proud of itself and might say, "I am so strong and powerful!" If it's a small wave, it may feel insecure or jealous of other waves. "I am so small and weak. I wish I were as fast or tall as the others!" The wave sets up various relationships to the other waves. It becomes close to a few of the neighboring waves, friendly with some, while others are mere acquaintances. There are some waves, too, that it doesn't like or doesn't want to be around.

We too suffer from the limitations of our identification with the body, mind, and intellect. We look at our appearance in the mirror and say, "I'm short," "I'm tall," or "I have long hair and brown eyes." About the state of our emotions, we say, "I'm happy," "I'm mad," or "I'm frustrated." About our thoughts, we say, "I understand this," "I'm confused," or "I doubt that this is true."

We look for fulfillment in the world of objects, emotions, and thoughts: With the body, we acquire and indulge in objects that please our senses.

Emotionally, we seek love and happiness through our relationships and interactions with things and beings around us. Intellectually, we enjoy having and using our knowledge, and also learning new knowledge. All these are expressions of our sense of individuality.

Individual ocean waves rise up, remain for a time, and then die away. But there is no birth and death for the ocean. Similarly, birth and death are only for the limited individual. So long as the sense of individuality exists, the soul journeys from lifetime to lifetime, taking on different bodies, personalities, and relationships until it fulfills its ultimate purpose of realizing its oneness with spirit.[8]

Om

All that is past, present, and future is verily Om.
—*Mandukya Upanishad*, 1.1

Now let's take a deeper look at *Om*. Gurudev explains, "*Om* represents the Self, which is the supreme, non-dual Reality."[9] It's the one essence or Self in all creation. It is called *God* in religion. *Om* is also referred to as *Supreme Consciousness, Supreme Self, Ultimate Cause,* or *Ultimate Truth.* The words *Supreme*

---

[8] Tejomayananda, *Amrtabindu Upanishad*, 49.
[9] Chinmayananda, *Meditation and Life*, 86.

and *Ultimate* tell us that there's nothing else beyond it or superior to it. It's the final and fundamental reality. Hence *Om* is placed at the top of the chart.

In the analogy of the ocean and waves, the ocean is not the ultimate reality of the waves. There's an even higher truth to it: "The true nature of the ocean is water; the waves, the foam, the sparkling ripples, and the flickering bubbles are all merely its various names and forms, having no separate individuality in themselves."[10] Just as water is the essential reality of the ocean and all its expressions, *Om* is the essential reality of all things and beings in creation. They have no separate existence apart from it.[11] You and I are different expressions of *Om*, the Ultimate Cause of all. As Gurudev puts it, "*Om* is the name of my own Self—my true name."[12]

Why is *Om* taken as a symbol for the Ultimate Cause? In Sanskrit, the sound of the letter *O* is made up of the vowels *A* and *U*. So the word *Om* can be broken down into three sounds, *A-U-M*. If you open your mouth slightly and make a sound without moving your mouth, tongue, or lips, "aaa" will be the sound you make. It arises from the throat, at the root of the tongue. When the "aaa" sound is sustained

---

[10] Ibid., 33.

[11] Ibid.

[12] Chinmayananda, *"Say Cheese!,"* 26.

and brought forward into the mouth, it results in the "uuu" sound. The sound ends by putting the lips together and producing the "mmm" sound.[13] When pronounced together, *A-U-M* make the sound *Om*. Since all sounds can be produced only in the space of the mouth from the root of the tongue to the lips, the letters *A-U-M* represent all possible sounds.[14]

Om comprises not only *A-U-M* but also the underlying silence. "Aaa" emerges from silence, "uuu" is sustained in silence, and "mmm" merges back into silence. Silence is the independent, underlying support of all three sounds. Even when they are not voiced, what endures is silence.[15]

Since *A-U-M* represent the emergence, sustenance, and dissolution of all possible sounds, they also symbolize the emergence, sustenance, and dissolution of creation."It [*Om*] is the Truth or the Self from which creation emerges, in which it exists and into which it merges."[16]

Thus *Om* is a suitable symbol for the underlying support and essence that pervades all creation, which is also our true nature.

---

[13] Swami Vivekananda, "The Mantra: Om: Word and Wisdom," quoted in Chinmayananda, *Meditation and Life*, 88.

[14] Ibid.

[15] Chinmayananda, *Meditation and Life*, 87.

[16] Tejomayananda, *Amrtabindu Upanishad*, 33.

Vasanas

Learn how to dissolve the vasanas and remove the ignorance that separates you from the effulgent flow of divinity into your life—and you will transcend the body-mind-intellect equipment to realize your true nature, Om.
—Swami Chinmayananda, *Self-Unfoldment*

The letter *V* in the chart represents the Sanskrit word *vasana* (pronounced *VAA-sa-naa*). Whenever we act with egocentric desires, impressions are laid in our minds that create tendencies to act in that same way again and again.[17] These tendencies are known as *vasanas.* They are hidden in our unconscious and direct the way we think, feel, and act.

Here's an example of how *vasanas* are formed. Let's say you smell a stick of jasmine incense for the very first time. If you enjoy it, an impression that jasmine incense is something pleasant is imprinted in your mind. If you're turned off by the smell, an impression that jasmine incense is not something that you like is created. Just as the fragrance lingers after the incense has burnt away, these mental impressions linger in your mind. In fact, the word *vasana* itself means "fragrance."[18] Every time the experience is repeated, or whenever you replay

---

[17] Chinmayananda, *Self-Unfoldment*, 103.

[18] Ibid., 39.

the memory of that experience in your mind, those impressions are strengthened. These become your *vasanas*. So if you liked the fragrance, you'll have a tendency to light and similarly enjoy incense in the future. If you disliked it, you'll want to stay away from it.

Your attraction or aversion to jasmine incense is an example of the expression of only one *vasana*. We all have a vast storehouse of innumerable *vasanas* from the thoughts and actions that we have done in this life, and all our previous lives. They are like millions of different seeds that we have planted. We can't see them, and we don't know which ones will sprout next. When they appear, they give rise to desires to gain something that we don't have or want more of in our lives. These desires push us to perform actions to achieve what we want. When we experience the results of our actions, they either place new impressions or reinforce previous ones— which start the cycle all over again. *Vasana* > desire > action > result > *vasana* > desire > action > result . . . ad infinitum.

Vasanas are the motivating force behind all our habits and behaviors. To illustrate how they express as our character and behavior, consider the example of Sally, a massage therapist who decided to treat herself to a solo vacation in the Caribbean. Just like anyone else planning a vacation, she arranged it based on what she wanted to do and enjoy there. Vedanta refers to our personal preferences as our likes and dislikes. They are expressions of our *vasanas*. As she wanted to have a quiet getaway, she chose a smaller hotel away from the touristy downtown area. She also opted for a garden-view room far from the main pool. She enjoyed eating the large variety of salads set out on the buffet table every day and drank only fresh fruit juices and water. She booked a couple of ecotours to enjoy the natural beauty of the island, and spent the rest of the time reading mystery novels by the beach. She was friendly with the people whom she met and enjoyed some pleasant conversations. All of Sally's choices, activities, thoughts, emotional reactions, and physical actions stemmed from her *vasanas*. *Vasanas* literally shape our personalities. If *you* had to plan *your* vacation, what choices would *you* make? They would all reflect your *vasanas*.

The pressure of our *vasanas* keeps pushing us out into the world to gain happiness, so we're unable to look within ourselves where real happiness lies. *Om*, our true nature, is the very wellspring of happiness. We need not struggle to gain it from the outer world, where it is not. To regain our true nature as the pure Self, we need to continually redirect our attention away from the world of objects, emotions, and thoughts and place it on an awareness of the Self. "When we identify with the Higher in us, the lower automatically drops away."[19] For example, when we mature into adults, our fascination for our childhood toys and games wears off on its own.

Vasanas are formed and perpetuated by our ignorance of our true nature. In Sanskrit, they're described as *avidya*, or ignorance.[20] It's this ignorance that veils the divinity within us and prevents us from realizing our true nature. This is why the letter *V* is placed between *Om* and the rest of the letters on the chart.

What's key to remember is that *only* actions motivated by self-centered desires create *vasanas*. Selfless actions done for the benefit of others or dedicated to an ideal, cause, or God prevent the formation of *vasanas* and slowly exhaust them.[21] As the *vasanas* are exhausted, the mind becomes quieter and starts to reflect the divinity within.

---

[19] Ibid., 40.
[20] Ibid., 41.
[21] Ibid., 104.

Here's a summary of the chart:

Om functioning through *Vasanas* identifies with Body > Perceiver > Objects.

Om functioning through *Vasanas* identifies with Mind > Feeler > Emotions.

Om functioning through *Vasanas* identifies with Intellect > Thinker > Thoughts.

Once you grasp the concepts in this chapter, you'll find it easier to step back and identify the aspect of your personality that is functioning at a given moment. For example, if you suddenly feel like having a cup of coffee or tea, know that your *vasana* for it is manifesting. When you make plans and organize your day, you are using your intellect. If you feel excited or frustrated about what you'll be doing, it's your mind that's expressing those emotions. If you're at a gathering and are aware of yourself as an individual in a roomful of others, you're asserting your ego, the perceiver-feeler-thinker personality. At every moment you are gleaning your life experiences through objects, emotions, and thoughts.

Remind yourself that your *vasanas,* intellect, mind, body, ego, objects, emotions, and thoughts are not you and belong to the world of matter. Shift your focus away from them all to your true nature, spirit, *Consciousness*, or *Om* that is beyond them all.

The spiritual journey is like playing a game of hide-and-seek. Spirit "hides" while you seek it. You look for it everywhere outside of yourself, never finding it, until one day, you decide to try a different strategy and search for it within yourself. This is where you will finally find it. When you do, you will realize a strange thing—the personality "you" never existed, and spirit was the only player.

CHAPTER 6

Vedanta

*Just as physics, biology, etc., are not the
exclusive property of any one country or people,
of a particular era or age, but are universally
applicable, irrespective of time and age, so too,
the Science of Living as propounded by the rishis
[sages] in Vedanta, visualizes a plan of life to
suit all people at all times and everywhere.*
—Swami Chinmayananda, *Kindle Life*

From Seeker to Sage

Vedanta is an ancient wisdom tradition that
originates from the inspired revelations of
great Himalayan sages. They taught these spiritual
teachings to their disciples, who then taught them
to their disciples. The teaching lineage that began
is very much alive even today. My guru, Swami
Chinmayananda, was a teacher from such a lineage
of spiritual masters.

There are no definitive sources that can put an
exact date to the origin of Vedanta. Since very little

is known about the background of the great sages or even their names, I often wondered how the first sage became a sage? What were the circumstances that led up to his spiritual seeking? One day I sat down and wrote a story about how this may have happened . . .

Picture a village at the southernmost tip of India, long before the growth of modern civilization. It was nestled in a lush valley, by the sparkling waters of a river. The people of the village lived peacefully off the land and the water. In that village was born a precocious child named Dheera. In Sanskrit, his name meant "the intelligent one" or "the one endowed with spiritual qualities."

From a very young age, Dheera proved to be very different from the other playful children of the village. He was profoundly moved by the wondrous beauty of nature around him. When the other children urged him to join them in play, he would invariably fall away from the group, being easily distracted by something that he heard or saw. If he saw a trail of ants, he would curiously follow them. The sight of a spider weaving a web, a butterfly landing on a flower, a glistening dewdrop on a leaf, or a bird in its nest would be enough to draw him into a whole new world, where the other children's happy laughter and loud calls faded away.

As he grew older, Dheera noticed that there was perfection and a precise order and intelligence in the world. The morning sun always rose over the river valley, casting shimmering light beams over the water, and set in the hills behind his village. The seed from a particular plant always produced an identical plant. The animals and birds instinctively knew what to eat, when to breed, and how to protect themselves from harm. There was symmetry and perfection in every flower and blade of grass. The bees always made hives with identical hexagonal cells and spiders always wove perfect webs.

He wondered, "There is so much beauty and intelligence around me! What is this world I live in? Where do the sun, moon, seas, rivers, creatures, trees, and vast sky come from? Who is the creator of all of these?" He asked his parents and the elders in his village, but no one seemed to have any answers. They told him that they had merely found themselves in this world. They did not know where it came from or who the creator was. They simply accepted things as they were, and they didn't understand why Dheera wasn't able to do the same.

As he grew into a teenager, Dheera became increasingly dissatisfied with life. He observed that people lived without any great purpose other than seeing to their basic daily needs and taking care of their families their entire lives. What was the point of it all? Did life have a higher purpose? Why was he here?

One day, as he sat by the banks of the river staring intensely into its depths, Dheera realized that he had outgrown life in the little village. Boldly, he stood up. He made a firm decision—he would leave his home to seek out the creator! Once he found him, he would ask him how he had created this world and what the purpose of life was.

When Dheera told his parents of his decision, they were shocked. Although they had noticed his growing restlessness, they did not expect him to leave the village altogether. Where would he go? They did not know very much of the world beyond their village and feared that he would not come back. "Don't go, Dheera. You'll never find what you're looking for!" they pleaded over and over again. But he didn't budge, standing tall and straight with unshakable determination.

The very next morning, carrying some simple tools and supplies, Dheera bid his parents farewell and walked fearlessly into the dense forest to the north of the village. With a premonition that they would never see their son again, his parents nervously watched him walk into the vast unknown. Dheera didn't look back.

He walked for many months. As he covered vast areas of the country, he saw the same hand of the creator everywhere: the same sun, moon, stars, sky, and clouds. The trees, birds, and animals were of different species, but they were nonetheless still trees, birds, and animals. However, the creator was still nowhere to be found. Dheera came across many villages where he asked people the same question: "Do you know where this world has come from?" They all looked at him as if he were mad.

The months turned into years, and Dheera continued walking north. Then, one day, as he looked ahead, he gasped. Before him were the tallest and most beautiful mountains he had ever seen. They were the mighty Himalayas. In all his travels, he had never seen such a majestic sight. As he looked up toward them, he instinctively knew that it was there he would find the answers he was seeking. Excitedly, he continued his journey north.

Dheera loved the mountains and lived there for many years, searching in caves, valleys, and forests for clues to the source of the world. Although he had no success, he never gave up. He was convinced that the creator, having the infinite power to create any environment and the freedom to live anywhere, would reside in no more splendid a place than in these mountains.

One night, Dheera couldn't sleep. He was tormented by memories of his last day with his parents. He remembered how shocked they were when he told them about his decision to leave. Their words "Don't go, Dheera. You'll never find what you're looking for!" echoed in his head. Now sounding like a cruel self-fulfilling prophecy, they overwhelmed him with a profound sense of dejection and failure. Deeply distraught, he tossed and turned, as an unrelenting stream of self-condemning thoughts whipped him into an exhausted stupor. Finally, he fell asleep.

When he woke up, it was minutes before dawn. Still groggy and unfocused, he staggered to the top of a large, flat rock on the mountainside overlooking a deep valley. As he stood there, he realized that his entire life had been a fruitless and insane search for the impossible. The clues that the creator existed were all around him, yet the creator remained maddeningly elusive. Feeling utterly hopeless, Dheera decided that life was not worth living. He would throw himself off the side of the mountain and kill himself!

Haltingly, he moved to the edge of the rock. He leaned forward slowly, inch by inch, passively waiting for the moment when the weight of his upper body would tip him over into the dark abyss below.

Suddenly, something caught his attention. He stopped and quickly straightened his body. There, in front of him, he saw the spectacular orange rays of the rising sun peeking from behind the mountains. As the luminous orb rose, he stood there, mesmerized. Even though he had seen numerous beautiful sunrises, to his disturbed mind, it appeared as if this might be the most breathtaking sunrise of his life. He was overcome with a feeling of awe and reverence. He couldn't do it—he couldn't end his life. He stepped away from the edge, dropped to his knees and looked up with his arms stretched out. His entire being cried out with the burning questions that had consumed him since he was a child: "Who are you? Where are you? I have to know!"

Suddenly, he sat up very still and straight. He felt chills all over his body, and the hair on his limbs stood on end. He closed his eyes and spontaneously slipped into a vast meditative state. Out of that pristine inner silence, words started pouring into his mind:

> *I am without hands and legs, of incomprehensible power. I see without eyes, hear without ears. [I am] devoid of all forms . . .*[1]

---

[1] Chinmayananda, *Kaivalya Upanishad*, 1.1.21, 76.

*I am smaller than the smallest and also am I the
most vast. I am the manifold universe . . .* [2]

*In me alone everything is born; in me alone does
everything exist and in me alone gets everything
dissolved. . .* [3]

The words revealed the nature of the creator and
the world. They came in the form of a steady stream
of metrical chants called *mantras*. They infused every
cell of his body, nourishing him like ambrosia from
above. Dheera lost all track of time . . .

Later, as he slowly opened his eyes and came
out of that quiet state, he was astonished by what
he had experienced. Gratitude flooded his heart and
tears flowed down his cheeks. Instinctively, he knew
that there was much more to know. And so he sat in
meditation daily.

One day, in the stillness and serenity of the
predawn hours, Dheera transcended time and space
and glided into unfathomable depths within himself.
In a glorious inner realization, he recognized his
true spiritual essence—he was pure spirit, separate
and untouched by the human identity known as
Dheera. He was beyond all its imperfections, desires,

---

[2] Ibid., 1.1.20, 72.
[3] Ibid., 1.1.19, 70.

disease, suffering, and mortality.[4] Just as rivers lose their names and forms when they merge into the sea, having gone beyond the limitations of his ego, he found himself one with the Self, the supreme divinity and cause of the universe.[5] He became "The All."[6]

The creator and support of the world was not to be found outside but experienced within himself as *his own true Self*! *He* was what he had been seeking his entire life!

Dheera achieved what is known as Self-realization or liberation. He was permanently freed from the sorrows that arose from his identification with his human personality. From then on, he spent his life in meditation.

The story of how Dheera achieved the goal of his life and became a wise sage ends here. But I'll continue to use him as an example to illustrate how Vedanta developed . . .

A Teaching Tradition Begins

The village folk living in the mountains came to know of Dheera. His wise and benign appearance

---

[4] Chinmayananda, *Meditation and Life,* 31.

[5] Chinmayananda, *Mundaka Upanishad,* 3.2.8, 167.

[6] Chinmayananda, *Meditation and Life,* 31.

attracted not only their curiosity but also their respect. Slowly, many spiritual seekers who had the same earnest questions about life found their way to Dheera. "O Wise One, please tell us what is the cause of this world? How can we gain true happiness?" they asked.

Dheera explained that there is one Supreme Cause. It is Infinite, Changeless, and Eternal. "[It] is subtler than the subtlest and greater than the greatest. [It] is seated in the cavity of the heart of each living being. He who is free from willing and wishing, with his mind and senses composed, beholds the majesty of the Self, and becomes free from sorrow."[7] This was their ultimate goal and the way to permanent happiness.

A handful of serious and dedicated seekers had a burning desire to gain firsthand knowledge of the Self and be liberated from the sorrows of life. They renounced all their worldly ties and asked Dheera if he would be their teacher. Seeing their sincere thirst for truth, Dheera compassionately agreed. They called him "Guru Dheera." In Sanskrit, the root *gu* means "darkness" and *ru* means "remover of."[8] Taken together in this way, the word *guru* refers to

---

[7] Chinmayananda, *Katha Upanishad,* 1.2.20, 115–16.

[8] Ishwarananda, *Guru Stotram,* 9.

the one who removes the darkness of ignorance with the light of knowledge.

Guru Dheera provided his disciples with loving but strict guidance conducive to the blossoming of the noble qualities of the head and heart. These were necessary for the seekers to achieve their goal. Their minds were developed with the right knowledge of life and the truth. As their vision expanded, noble virtues such as love, compassion, forgiveness, humility, and contentment grew in their hearts. This inner nurturing was a very slow and painstaking process. The guru had great love and endless patience. Gurudev describes the relationship between a guru and his disciples as that of a gardener and the flowers in a bush. The gardener does not create the flowers. He takes care of the bush, providing water, sunlight, protection, fertilizer, and pruning. The bush, under the careful tending of the gardener, produces fragrant flowers on its own. The gardener lovingly facilitates the process.[9]

Guru Dheera taught them all that he knew. However, he could not bestow Self-realization. He warned, "Do not accept my words. There can be no illumination without your own intimate realization of the truth. Meditate and seek it within yourself!"

---

[9] Chinmayananda, *Penguin Swami Chinmayananda Reader*, 157–58.

Guru Dheera never asked for anything in return. His disciples, however, felt a deep sense of gratitude and reverence for their guru. They took it on themselves to serve his simple needs for food, water, and warmth. They spent their entire lives serving him and learning from him in an attitude of humility and surrender. To them, their guru was the embodiment of their goal. They saw him as "nothing but pure consciousness, absolute bliss [and] eternal wisdom."[10]

In time, following the guru's instructions, one or two of his best students achieved Self-realization. When Guru Dheera left his physical body, these disciples became the next generation of teachers for other seekers with the same timeless questions. Each guru taught his students the *mantras* that he had learned from his teacher and added the *mantras* that were revealed to him in his own meditation. In this way, the body of knowledge grew over succeeding generations.

Since this teaching tradition predates the time when people learned to write, the knowledge was communicated in an oral form. The guru repeated the *mantras* to his disciples, which they chanted and memorized every day. The guru then expounded on their subtle meaning and significance. Each guru

---

[10] Chinmayananda, *Kena Upanishad,* 52.

taught in a way that was relevant and applicable to the spiritual seekers of his time.

This method of direct learning from the mouth of the guru demanded an acute intelligence and a tenacious memory. The teachers only accepted students of the highest caliber. Blind belief and mechanical repetition had no place in the communication of knowledge between the teacher and his students. The disciples were expected to dialogue with the guru and ask questions to dispel all their doubts. No question was unimportant or went unanswered. They were then required to reflect independently and meditate deeply on the guru's teachings.[11]

Along with a deep desire to discover the truth, the students also had to have an unflinching faith in and devotion to their guru. The inner journey to the truth was not an easy one, and there were many dangers and pitfalls along the way. Faith in the words of the guru was critical in keeping the seekers on track and inspired to continue. They also had to be willing to undergo rigorous self-discipline as prescribed by their guru. The ultimate goal of life was not to be gained by the undisciplined and

---

[11] You can read about this process in the section "Three Steps to Reveal the Self" in chapter 10.

faint-hearted. The guru's constant guidance was vital to their success.

The Vedas and Vedanta

The spiritual masters were great scientists of life. "While material scientists take the outer world as their field of investigation, the subjective scientists [the spiritual masters] take their own inner world of experiences as the field of their search for truth."[12] The scope and depth of their intense meditations is mind-boggling.

They intuited the nature of the Supreme Reality and the means to reach it. They unraveled the most profound secrets of the cosmos from the smallest and subtlest form of matter to the vast sun, stars, planets, moons, and ever-expanding universes. Focusing on humans, they examined all three states of consciousness that we go through daily—the waking, dream, and deep sleep states. They detected the different layers of the human personality and examined each one. They discerned the inner workings of the mind, conscious and subconscious imprints and desires, the energy body, and the physical body. They discovered the nature and source of the ego. They apprehended the cause of

---

[12] Chinmayananda, *Self-Unfoldment*, 19.

suffering and prescribed the art of living for people of different temperaments. To these great scientists, a person's experiences in a specific embodiment did not give a full understanding of life. They scrutinized life before birth and after death, and discovered the cause of rebirth.

As the centuries progressed and populations grew, more and more people needed help and guidance in their everyday lives. The masters turned no one away. They gave instructions on various actions and rituals to perform for the fulfillment of specific desires. They taught various spiritual disciplines and subtler methods of worship and meditation.

At first, all the knowledge was transferred verbally from the guru to his disciples. At some point in the history of man, it was organized, compiled, written down and preserved into four great books called the *Vedas*. The four *Vedas* are *Rg Veda, Sama Veda, Yajur Veda,* and *Atharva Veda*.[13] This herculean task is credited to the efforts of one spiritual giant— Sage Vyasa. Because of this, he is referred to as Veda Vyasa. "The word, *Veda* is derived from the Sanskrit root *vid*, 'to know.' Thus *Veda* came to mean 'knowledge of the Truth.' Just as God and the creation are infinite and eternal, so also *Veda* or knowledge

---

[13] Ibid., 152.

of God [Truth] is infinite and exists eternally in the universe."[14]

The most sublime knowledge of the *Vedas* is the knowledge of the Self. It is found in the concluding portions of the *Vedas* called the *Upanishads*. These are the teachings and discussions on Self-knowledge conducted by the gurus in answer to the questions posed by the students.

The word *Upanishad* comes from three root words: *upa, ni,* and *shad.* The word *upa* means to go "near" or approach a guru with faith and devotion. *Ni* signifies the "determined practice" of the knowledge that one gains from the teacher. And *shad* means "to destroy." The meaning of *Upanishad* itself conveys the process of gaining the knowledge of the Self: When a sincere student approaches a guru (*upa*) for spiritual knowledge, the guru teaches him or her. Having gained it, the student makes it his or her own through a determined practice (*ni*) of meditation. This destroys (*shad*) the student's ignorance, and leads him or her to the realization of the Self.[15]

You may be wondering what all this has to do with Vedanta. The word *Vedanta* is broken into *veda* (knowledge) and *anta* (end), meaning the "end

---

[14] Ibid.

[15] Tejomayananda, *Upanishad Course*, lesson 1.

portion of the *Vedas*."[16] Vedanta refers to the science of the Self found in the *Upanishads* that are at the end of the *Vedas*. However, this literal meaning isn't the only meaning of *Vedanta*. *Vedanta* also means "The end (or the goal) of knowledge."[17]

The goal of all knowledge is the knowledge of the Self. It is also the supreme goal of life because with the knowledge or realization of our own infinite and blissful nature, there will be nothing more to know, accomplish, or have. It will bring us the consummation of all our desires and an absolute fulfilment in life.[18] This will put a permanent end to all our sorrows and striving for happiness. The teachings of Vedanta are, therefore, wisdom for all humankind.

---

[16] Chinmayananda, *Self-Unfoldment*, 153.

[17] Ibid.

[18] Chinmayananda, *Taittiriya Upanishad*, 2.1.1, 140–41.

PART 2

Now What?

How to Live
as a Spiritual Being

*If you are not willing to change, do not enter the
path of spirituality.*

> —Swami Chinmayananda,
> *Final Score—Love All!*

CHAPTER 7

Birth of a Spiritual Seeker

The moment one questions the validity of the pursuits one has been following, one becomes a seeker.

—Swami Chinmayananda, *Unto Him*

Search for Happiness

We all have different desires and goals in life based on our interests and personalities. Although our individual goals vary, our underlying motive is the same. Through all our various pursuits, we are actually seeking happiness.[1] The people with whom we cultivate relationships, the work and the activities that we choose, the food we eat, where we live, what we buy—literally every decision and action is motivated by a desire to be happy. You're reading this book because you think you'll gain something from it, and this makes you happy.

When something no longer gives us the

---

[1] Chinmayananda, *Self-Unfoldment*, 26.

satisfaction or joy that we are seeking, we replace it with something else that we think will. So if your household appliances and other devices don't work as efficiently as they used to or break down, you buy new ones. If your city or town doesn't give you the security or satisfaction you want, you move. If your relationships with people in your life are strained or unhappy, you look for others to make you happy. When you can't replace the people in your life, you look for ways to keep your present relationships happy.

We love being happy and can't stand being unhappy. What's more, we don't want our experience of happiness to be interrupted or lacking. We are not satisfied with being happy *some* of the time or being *somewhat* happy. We want to be *absolutely happy, all the time*. But the truth is that no outer joy fulfills us completely, and our happiness keeps slipping away. Dissatisfaction, disappointment, sorrow, and suffering show up uninvited and interrupt our experience of happiness. This happens because of three changing factors:

1. *The world.* Something or the other changes and puts an end to the happiness that we experience. For example, your neighbor's daughter whom you happily trusted to babysit your children can no longer do so because she has gone to university

in another city. Or, you used to enjoy the peaceful atmosphere around your apartment when you moved in ten years ago, but the construction of new buildings around you has spoiled your view and quietude. Or, the furniture and fittings that you considered fashionable years ago now look worn-out and shabby.

2. *Our minds.* Very often, even if things, circumstances, and people haven't changed, they don't give us the same happiness as before because *we* change our minds about them. For instance, you relished the food at your favorite restaurant and ate there every week. But now you're tired of it. Your once perfect job doesn't satisfy you anymore, and you start looking for another one that does. The city lifestyle that you used to thrive on now aggravates you, and you want to move to the suburbs.

3. *Our desires.* After we acquire something, the joy that arose when we first got it soon becomes stale. This is because a fresh set of desires sprouts in our mind. For example, you've taken a long flight to be in the peaceful mountains with your partner. And now, you're finally there, sitting on the balcony of your hotel room happily enjoying the beautiful view. Within a very short time, you begin to feel restless. Now that you're there and have experienced the view, what else is there to do? You run back inside and

bring out all the brochures on the local attractions that you had picked up from the hotel lobby. You start planning the next activity that you can enjoy—perhaps a hike, a bicycle ride, or a visit to the local market. Your numerous and changing desires crowd out the happiness that you were enjoying.

We take great pains to maintain a perfect arrangement of things, circumstances, and people around us to keep us happy. However, this carefully created setup is soon upset because either outer factors keep changing or, inwardly, our minds and desires keep changing. Invariably, something or the other changes and puts an end to the happiness that we were experiencing. To regain the lost happiness, we start searching for it in other ways. When we find it, we are happy—for some time that is, until things change, and then the search for happiness begins all over again.

What's strange is that even though we never find *the* thing, person, place, or situation that will keep us permanently happy, we never stop looking for it. We seem to be convinced that the perfect happiness is out there.

The truth is that real happiness isn't "out there" but "in here" within us. Dheera (from chapter 6), who gained a firsthand experience of his true Self, found total bliss and contentment in life. *We* are the source of all happiness and what we are really searching for. Not knowing this, we continually look for happiness in the outer world. But it's impossible to find permanent happiness in a world that is in itself impermanent. As we learn more about the real source of happiness that lies within us and strive to know it, we will begin to enjoy a more satisfying and lasting happiness.

Inner Stirrings

Despite being frustrated at not being able to find the perfect happiness, most people don't seek anything higher or more out of life. They may not know that there is something more. And so they continue to look for worldly solutions to their worldly problems, never seeking out spiritual possibilities. Let's say someone is dissatisfied with the amount of money she's making or is not able to find the right job or a happy, fulfilling relationship. Like most people, she would be happy if she made more money, or if her career took off, or if she found a partner who fulfills her. When we experience sorrow, we try to get rid of it by pursuing another source of joy from the world itself. As long as we are satisfied with this and don't question it, we'll keep doing it. There would be no searching for anything higher at this stage of our growth.

But there are some people who are beginning to hear the inner voice of their true Self. They are feeling a growing dissatisfaction with worldly joys and gains, and the never-ending efforts to achieve them. They are looking for something that will bring them greater fulfillment. These are people who are at the threshold of spirituality.

A person who is ready may have what looks like a happy and comfortable life on the outside—a good job, enough money, a loving family, great friends, a nice house, a car, and so on. Or, someone may neither have all those things nor have a desire for them. Outer wealth and accomplishments have no bearing on an inner readiness for spirituality. The first person may ask, "Why am I not happy in spite of having so much? What am I missing?" The second one may question materialistic goals and worldly values and ask, "What else could there be?" In both these cases, it's an inner awakening to the temporary and intrinsically unsatisfactory nature of worldly things and relationships. They both want more out of life but don't know where to begin their search. They go from one thing to the next, continuously looking for new objects, people, and experiences in the hope of finding the fulfillment they are looking for. They may find something that distracts them temporarily, but sooner or later, the same feeling of lack and incompleteness nags at them again.

It's similar to what happens when a baby cries because she has an upset stomach. All she knows is that something is hurting inside. And all she can do is cry. Her frantic mother changes her diaper, loosens her clothes, and gives her colorful toys to play with. These may distract her momentarily, but the baby soon starts crying again. What she's feeling is deep inside her belly, and changing things from the outside cannot take away that pain.

Waking Up

If you have felt this inner unease but find that this feeling of discomfort is mild or comes only rarely, you may ignore it and tell yourself that everything is fine, and there's no reason to feel this way. And so you get right back into your normal life and preoccupations. This is what we usually do when the Self comes calling. But the Self has infinite patience. It waits for the perfect opportunity to nudge us again.

Luckily, there is no dearth of opportunities to wake us up to the divine inner call. A serious illness, the loss of a job or a cherished relationship, a financial blow, or the death of a loved one can trigger the spiritual seeking. Some people naturally start reflecting on their lives as they age. They may be divorced, retired, or empty nesters looking for meaning in their lives. The wisest are those who start thinking about their own lives after observing the challenges and failures of others. In all these situations, something "clicks" inside, and they start to turn inward. Remember Lori from the first chapter? High levels of stress and health concerns drew her into the spiritual life. In my own case, the shock of losing my father from a heart attack when he was just fifty-four pushed me to seek answers to the nature of death and the journey of the soul. It was then that I started looking for a guru to guide me and explain life to me.[2]

Diving In

No matter the circumstances that bring you to the threshold of your spiritual life, once you're there, you may be interested in learning more about religion and spirituality, self-improvement, healing modalities, or alternative medicine. You expand your thinking through books, magazines, articles, and the internet. You may seek guidance from others

---

[2] You can read about my personal journey and how I met my guru, Swami Chinmayananda, in the appendix.

more knowledgeable than you who can answer your questions about life.

As you gain greater insight on life, you understand that we all put in great efforts to acquire, enjoy, and preserve money, possessions, skills, worldly achievements, and relationships in the face of many challenges and hardships. In the process, we go through a roller coaster of joys and sorrows, experiencing love, fear, elation, depression, peace, anxiety, joy, grief, anger, and so on. And then—we die, and the whole drama mysteriously disappears! We leave everything behind. The tragic irony is that we also leave our bodies behind. Why do and gain anything when everything eventually comes to naught? What is the real purpose of life? Why is there suffering? Where does real happiness lie? When you seriously start seeking answers to these fundamental questions, you become a spiritual seeker. There is really no birth into the spiritual life without this sincere inner longing for answers.

In the light of this new awakening, you begin to scrutinize your priorities and pursuits. Worldly values begin to crumble away. Achieving materialistic goals becomes less important or fulfilling. Instead of focusing on "What's in it for me?" you begin to ask, "How can I serve and give to others?" You look for ways to use your skills and talents to help others around you in your home, workplace, or community.

As with Lori, your new spiritual view will spread to all areas of your life. You may clean and reorganize your house or work space. This is very common. When you revamp your life, you can't help but want to clean up your physical space too. You start cutting back on the activities and things that are not in alignment with your new goal of growing spiritually. You naturally reduce the time you spend on activities such as watching TV and movies, playing games or surfing the internet, or engaging with social media. Your interest in shopping, clothes, shoes, cars, late nights, parties, the latest gadgets, and traveling starts to dwindle. You spend more time on things that promote the health of your body and mind. You may start to learn meditation. You exercise regularly, eat healthier, natural, or organic foods and cut back on or avoid meat and alcohol. You are now more careful in caring for yourself, others, and the environment. And so you choose all-natural products for your personal care, home, and work.

You do your utmost to nurture positive relationships with your friends, family, and others while honoring yourself. You discreetly withdraw from people who don't reflect your values and forge meaningful relationships with people who do. You are more careful of maintaining integrity in what you think, say, and do. What others think of you is not as important as being able to live up to your own conscience.

Cultivating a spiritual vision, shifting your priorities, and making positive changes in your life takes time. Inner growth happens slowly and organically. In the beginning, even though you may value your spiritual goals, you may not be ready to totally leave behind your attachments to the things and people that you enjoy. Old habits die hard.

But, as you persevere with consistency and faith, you slowly wean yourself off your dependence on people, things, and situations for your happiness, and start tapping into a deeper, more satisfying joy. The new habits gradually become a part of your character and your life. You'll finally be on your way to gaining the *real* happiness that you are searching for.

In the following chapters I present the core practices and mind-set of a spiritual seeker.

CHAPTER 8

Embarking on Your Spiritual Journey

In life, we cannot expect to be completely free of
worldly entanglements; to wait for such a time
before we undertake the spiritual path is absurd.
It is like waiting for the waves to subside before
taking a swim in the sea.
—Swami Chinmayananda, *Self-Unfoldment*

If you've arrived at a stage in your life where you are sincerely ready to embark on your spiritual journey, you are to be applauded. You are among a small but growing number of people who are seeing life from a spiritual perspective. You don't want to wait any longer for the "perfect" time to embark on your spiritual journey. You are becoming what I call a "Conscious Evolver."

There are three practices that will support your growth on your journey: keeping spiritual company, reflection, and daily introspection.

Satsang—Keeping Spiritual Company

We can think of satsang as a fortress we build around ourselves to protect us against the temptations that we encounter in our daily lives.
—Swami Chinmayananda, *Self-Unfoldment*

To grow spiritually and to maintain that growth, it's very important to keep your mind uplifted through regular *satsang*. *Satsang* is a Sanskrit word made up of two root words, *sat* and *sang*. *Sat* means "truth," "good," or "noble." *Sang* means "in the company of" or "in association with." *Satsang* means being associated with the truth, or with that which is good and noble.[1] It means keeping spiritual company. This is "good" because it brings peace of mind, and "noble" because it promotes spiritual growth.

You can be in *satsang* in many ways: When you congregate with others to worship the divine, sing devotional hymns, listen to spiritual discourses, and read from holy books, this is being in *satsang*. If this is not your scene, then meeting with a friend or a few like-minded people to discuss spirituality and ways to promote your spiritual growth qualifies as *satsang*. On your own, you can partake of *satsang* by reading spiritual books, magazines, and articles. You

---

[1] Tejomayananda, *Satsanga*, 1.

can listen to inspirational spiritual speakers or their recordings. The internet is overflowing with videos, audios, and online events that can provide a healthy dose of *satsang*.

Satsang instills your mind with higher ideals and noble thoughts. This helps develop your sense of discernment in life. It supports your ability to judge between what is right and wrong, good and bad, your ultimate goal and what is only a means toward it, or even a distraction. *Satsang* is a vital discipline that will help to keep you inspired and on path.

Reflection

Both the head and heart must assimilate any new idea before it can really be our own. We hear or read the idea, then reflect on it until the light of understanding dawns in our own bosom.
— Swami Chinmayananda, *In the Company of Sages*

Taking your mind to *satsang* is the first important step, but to keep up the learning and inspiration, you have to bring the new ideas into your own life. Otherwise, *satsang* will provide only a temporary inspiration and not create any real change in you.

Have you heard or read an inspirational quotation that really touched your heart, but all too soon— sometimes within minutes—it was forgotten? It left a pleasant feeling and you *did* remember that it was a good one, but you can't seem to remember what it was about. Why did you forget it so easily? How can you firmly imprint life's lessons into your mind where they can transform you? The answer is daily reflection. Without it, your freshly inspired mind turns cold and dull again.

Once, Gurudev told a story about how in the homes of the poor in India, people used to cook over wood or coal fires. It was common for people to "borrow" some burning embers to start a quick fire instead of starting a new one from scratch. One day, a woman went to her neighbor to ask for some pieces of burning coal for her cooking. Not having a suitable container, she took with her a couple of sheets of *The Indian Express* newspaper to carry home the burning embers. She stood outside her neighbor's door as he dropped a few burning pieces into her flimsy, makeshift "container." Almost immediately, the scorching pieces of coal started to burn through the newspaper. By the time she got home, the coals had fallen to the ground, and all she was left with was a burnt-up mess of paper in her hands.

Gurudev laughed as he explained that our minds are like a copy of the daily newspaper—chock full of worldly excitements, news, and concerns. We get a "burning" idea or inspiration that touches us deeply, but because our minds are so preoccupied, the inspiration fizzles away very quickly. And we go on as before.

Take a few minutes every morning before you start your daily duties to read something uplifting, inspirational, or requiring deep thought. The morning is the best time for this because that's when the mind is quiet and receptive. Whatever you think about at that time will sink into your subconscious mind and color your thoughts and actions throughout your day. Try to get up a few minutes earlier to give yourself some private time for your daily reflection.

As an example of a quotation that you can reflect on, here's one of Gurudev's: *We do not realize that true freedom is built on intelligent self-restraint.*[2] You may read this quote with some surprise. Isn't freedom all about doing anything you want, whenever you want? If you can't do that, then that's not really being free, is it? But as you reflect deeper, you realize that you're not very good at imposing "self-restraint." You give in repeatedly to the demands of your senses and then regret it. The pull is irresistible. Maybe, you think back to the holidays two years ago when you overate and put on five pounds which you still haven't been able to take off. Or you remember when you gave in to the temptation of retaliating with hurtful words and strained a relationship.

---

[2] Chinmayananda, *Self-Unfoldment*, 2.

Why couldn't you control yourself? Are you really free, if you're not able to control your own mind and senses? You realize that no matter what kind of outer freedom you enjoy, you're not going to enjoy true freedom unless you can impose some "intelligent self-restraint."

Daily Introspection

Introspection, detection, negation, and substitution constitute the preliminary processes in the purification and tempering of the seeker.
—Swami Chinmayananda, *Meditation and Life*

Introspection takes your newly acquired skills in reflection to a deeper level. In this practice you take some time to review your day as an impartial witness, paying close attention to the motives behind your thoughts, words, and deeds. As you become aware of your true intentions while replaying the incidents in your mind, you will come to know the habits and behaviors that you need to give up, modify, or nurture. Introspection also prepares you to watch your thoughts with detachment in meditation. It is a practice that has great potential to positively transform your character. It consists of four steps: introspection, detection, negation, and substitution.[3]

Introspection

Begin your practice of introspection after dinner, when your day's responsibilities are over, and you're feeling relaxed. Find a quiet place where you can sit undisturbed for about ten to fifteen minutes. Breathe slowly and deeply.

Gently allow the memories of the day to float up into your consciousness. Look at them with as much detachment as you can. How did you respond to the circumstances and people with whom you met? How did your behavior affect those around you? What were the underlying motives and feelings behind your behavior and speech? Simply be aware of them.

Observing yourself like this is hard to do. We don't generally have enough detachment to see our own faults. Who we think we are is very different from who we actually are. While we may think we are right, good, honest, and fair, we may be totally the opposite. Our attachment to ourselves and our self-centered desires blind us to our own failings. It adds a false sense of beauty to our pursuits. When people point out our shortcomings, we become angry

---

[3] Chinmayananda, *Self-Unfoldment*, 85–86.

and defensive. We cover them up with lies or try to justify our behavior.

Detection

In the beginning, as you replay the events of your day, you may not see anything out of the ordinary. You may even look back and congratulate yourself for how well you handled things. After some days of practice, you will gain more detachment and thereby become sensitive to your own faults and shortcomings. For instance, you may realize that because of jealousy and insecurity in your own position, you failed to help a colleague at work. Or you spoke sweetly to someone and then criticized her behind her back. Did the argument with your partner occur because your ego was hurt?

The process of becoming aware of your real motives and character is called detection. As you can imagine, this isn't very pleasant. You may feel a sense of disappointment, guilt, or perhaps even shame. It's very important not to get stuck at this stage by allowing these feelings to debilitate your forward movement. Take them as pointers that show you where you can change.

Negation

If you have the courage and determination to advance spiritually, recognizing your faults will make you want to change immediately. In negation, you reject your false values, low thoughts, motives, and behavior while being very careful not to allow self-condemnation or self-blame to seep in. Stay positive and grateful that you have developed this level of self-awareness.

Substitution

Substitution completes the transformative process. Never move away from your practice without substituting the negative thoughts and behaviors with positive ones. Unless you do this, your introspection practice will erode your confidence, and you will become frustrated with yourself. Resolve to make changes and make sure you back them up with a solid plan of action.

Do this four-step process daily. Introspection will become easier and very rewarding. You'll begin to develop a distance between the ego you and the real you who is witnessing your life. The internal changes that you make will build up your self-esteem and integrity. Being aware of your inner world and staying true to your own ideals and values will be your ultimate measure of happiness. Introspection is an indispensable habit of a true spiritual seeker.

The Path of the Good and the Path of the Pleasant

Both the good and the pleasant approach the mortal man. The wise man examines them thoroughly and discriminates between the two. The wise man prefers the good to the pleasant; but the ignorant man chooses the pleasant for the sake of the body through avarice and attachment (for getting and keeping).
—*Katha Upanishad* 1.22

You can support your new habits of *satsang*, reflection, and introspection by making the right choices throughout the day. When meeting any challenge, you can choose between the Path of the Good and the Path of the Pleasant.[4]

Taking the Path of the Good may be difficult, unpleasant, or inconvenient. It requires making a sacrifice now but brings you happiness in the long run. The Path of the Pleasant is the easy path. It is attractive and convenient and brings you instant gratification, but sorrow in the long run. Gurudev compares them to two paths on a hillside.[5] The Path of the Pleasant is an easy, wide, and downhill path, lined with colorful flowers. Most travelers happily take this path, only to be frustrated to find that it

---

[4] Chinmayananda, *Self-Unfoldment*, 24–27. Unless otherwise stated, this section on the Path of the Good and the Path of the Pleasant is based on this source.

[5] Chinmayananda, *Katha Upanishad,* 65.

ends at a dark and dreary cave. On the other hand, the Path of the Good is a narrow, uphill path that is rocky and challenging to climb. But the few, strong travelers who take it are rewarded by a spectacular view of the surroundings.

Here's a scenario to illustrate choosing between the Path of the Good and the Path of the Pleasant: Terry is shopping at a department store that is having a great weekend sale. Seeing how low the prices are, she picks up more than twelve items of clothing for herself and her family. There are long lines of people at the checkout where she waits to pay for her purchases. Finally, she gets to the front of the line. The store associate scans the items and tells her the total amount that she has to pay. Terry is pleasantly surprised to see how reasonable her bill is. As she hands him her credit card though, she gets a vague feeling that something may be amiss. There could be a mistake on the bill. Not wanting to hold up the line by examining her receipt right there, she gathers her bags and goes back to her car. In the car, she begins to crosscheck her items with the receipt. She discovers that the store associate had missed scanning a pair of children's pants worth $13.99.

At that point, Terry has two choices—she could chalk up the mistake to good luck and drive away or go back and pay for the pants. Her first instinct tells her that she should pay for them, but the thought of battling the crowds and standing in line to pay turns her off. So she decides that she won't go back. "After all," she tells herself, "I didn't take them on purpose. I would've paid for them had they been on the bill." Even as she thinks in this way, she squirms uncomfortably in her seat. She knows paying for the pants is the right thing to do. She tries to cover up her uneasiness by justifying why she needn't go back to the store. "It's not my fault that the store associate missed scanning the pants. It's not a lot of money, anyway. At the end of the day, no one will ever know."

A little voice reminds her that even though her children were not with her, she had been teaching them to be honest. What kind of a role model would she be if she was saying one thing and doing the exact opposite? This thought empowers her. She sits up straight in her seat. "That's true! What a hypocrite I'd be!" She makes a firm decision that she *will* pay for the pants. She decides that she'll come back after the weekend sale when the store would be less busy. She'll go back home now, show her children her purchases and explain what happened. That would be the perfect opportunity to reinforce a lesson in honesty. Maybe she would even take them with her when she went back to the store.

Having made that decision, Terry felt strong and very good about herself. This was following the Path of the Good. Had she succumbed to the temptation of keeping the pants without paying for them, she would have taken the easy Path of the Pleasant.

Now, you may think that this example is too simple. Why didn't I give you an example where there would be a serious moral dilemma? This example of sticking to the Path of the Good in a trivial matter emphasizes that it's the small everyday decisions that form our character. As spiritual seekers striving to grow, it's important to think carefully about the short- and long-term effects of our big *and* small choices.

The Path of the Good is the path of spiritual evolution. It brings lasting peace and builds integrity of character. On the other hand, following the Path of the Pleasant brings immediate joy but weakens your resolve and keeps you attached to your body and worldly pleasures. This does not mean that you have to suppress your desires and live a dry, joyless life in order to grow spiritually. By gaining the right understanding and clarity about life and your spiritual goals through *satsang*, reflection, and introspection, you'll be able to sublimate your lower impulses and make higher choices. Then choosing the Good over the Pleasant will become easier, and always feel like the right choice for you.

CHAPTER 9

The Path of Action and the Path of Devotion

Perform every action as an act of divine worship without caring for its fruit. Thus make all actions pure [and] uncontaminated by the desire for reward.
—Swami Tapovanam,
Guidance from the Guru

Karma Yoga—the Path of Action

A path or means that helps us progress toward our union with the Self is called a *yoga*. The Sanskrit word *yoga* comes from the root word *yuj*, which means "to join."[1] A yoga is a means to grow spiritually. The masters of Vedanta prescribe three yogas for the three aspects of our personality:

Karma yoga, the Path of Action for the body.
Bhakti yoga, the Path of Devotion for the mind.
Jnana yoga, the Path of Knowledge for the intellect.

---

[1] Chinmayananda, *Self-Unfoldment*, 260.

120

The Right Actions

The word *karma* simply means "action." *Karma yoga* is the art of doing the right actions with the right attitude.[2] From the lowest to the highest, there are three types of actions: prohibited actions, desire-prompted actions, and obligatory duties.

Prohibited actions violate standards of what is universally considered good conduct. These actions harm others physically or emotionally. Examples include lying, cheating, stealing, and killing to protect one's own interests or for personal gain. This category of actions strengthens our negative tendencies and backfires as mental agitation in the form of remorse and fear. In addition, when caught, the wrongdoer has to suffer the physical consequences of his or her actions.

Next are desire-prompted actions, which are not prohibited. These are activities that we do for personal pleasure and entertainment such as indulging in our favorite foods, hobbies, traveling, watching sports, and so on.

Both prohibited actions and desire-prompted actions are driven by our *vasanas* which express themselves as our personal likes and dislikes.[3] These

---

[2] Tejomayananda, *Bhagavad Gita Course,* lesson 5. Unless otherwise stated, this is the source of the material for this section and the next.

[3] See the section on *vasanas* in chapter 5.

actions strengthen or add new *vasanas* to the load that we are already carrying. Because of this, the spiritual masters urge us to strictly avoid prohibited actions and to thoughtfully and gradually reduce our desire-prompted actions.

The right actions that we must do are our obligatory duties. We are required to perform our duties at home, at work, in our community, or for our country. They come to us as part and parcel of our roles and relationships with others such as being a parent, an employer or employee, resident in a community, or citizen of a nation. Duties are done to benefit others or for the common good of all. We are expected to fulfill our duties simply because they need to be done.

Most of these duties are done daily, but we may also be called to perform occasional duties. For instance, you may need to visit someone at the hospital or attend a funeral or a wedding. Or you may need to fulfill your duties as a volunteer at an annual fund-raising event for your favorite charity or do jury duty. Since duties are done for others, they help lessen our selfish tendencies and cleanse our mind of *vasanas.* This is the reason why daily and occasional duties must never be neglected.

The Right Attitude

More important than doing our duties is how we do them, because it's the right attitude that advances our spiritual growth. In *Karma yoga* we do our actions without attachment—neither to the work nor to the anticipated results.[4]

Attachment to the work means doing it with a sense of ego and allowing what you do and how you do it to be driven by your personal likes and dislikes. You may want to do only a specific job or task or do it only in a particular way. You may also be reluctant to give up or share the responsibilities with others because of a sense of possessiveness toward your position or fondness for the work.

Our duties entail doing many tasks, some of which we may dislike. We often want to do only what we enjoy and try to avoid or delay doing what we find difficult, inconvenient, or unpleasant. For example, a personal support worker, caring for the elderly in their homes, may love being with her clients and serving their needs but dislikes putting together the periodic reports required by the company that employs her. Consequently, the reports are often late or lacking all the necessary information. The company has to frequently remind her to submit them.

---

[4] Chinmayananda, *Holy Geeta*, 18.9, 1051.

We must fulfill *all* our prescribed duties readily, cheerfully, efficiently, and to the best of our ability. We shouldn't complain about what we have to do or do tasks grudgingly. Personal likes or dislikes should not stand in the way of doing our duties.[5] Instead, our actions must be guided by what we know is right and ought to be done.

Attachment to the anticipated results is an insistence that we get the results that we want.[6] For example, Susan is a floor supervisor at a manufacturing company. She knows that her manager will be retiring in the next three months and she'll be one of two people being considered for the position. She's anxious for the promotion not only because it will raise her status in the company but also because it will mean a significant increase in her salary. She puts in longer hours and works harder than before. She frequently imagines the general manager praising her heartily for her efforts before offering her the position. She feels excited knowing that she can use the extra money she'll get toward a down payment on an apartment of her own.

After a few weeks, the general manager calls her into his office. Susan knocks at his door with nervous anticipation. He smiles, shakes her hand,

---

[5] Ibid., 18.23, 1074.
[6] Ibid., 18.27, 1080.

and leads her inside. After a little pleasantry, he tells her that he's happy with the work that she has been doing. And so he's decided to offer her a promotion to *assistant* manager along with a modest increase in her salary. Susan is crushed. She tries her best to hide her disappointment and feigns a half-smile. She feels that all her efforts went to waste and thinks that he's being unfair, as she is the better candidate for the managerial position.

As she takes on her new responsibilities, bitter feelings constantly interrupt her mind from the work at hand. Her work begins to suffer, and she has frequent disagreements with her new manager. The general manager notices the change in her attitude. When another opportunity for a promotion opens up in the company a few months later, he doesn't consider her, as he feels she doesn't demonstrate good leadership skills and team spirit.

When practicing *karma yoga*, we give up the anxiety for the results of our actions. Results can be tangible, such as money, power, position, gifts, and favors, or intangible, such as praise, admiration, and appreciation. There should be no hankering for any rewards. Whatever the results, we accept them cheerfully without complaint. The only reward we seek is the satisfaction of doing the right job in the right way.

Susan in the example above worked with attachment. As a floor supervisor, she hankered for the position of manager, and as an assistant manager, she worked with strong personal likes and dislikes. Had she kept her focus on doing her best at her job, she could have advanced professionally and spiritually.

Gurudev sums up attachment as "Attachment = Ego + Egocentric desires."[7] Another way that he explains attachment is performing your actions with a sense of "I" + "I want."

Now, to perform your duties without attachment to the work or to the results requires a strong motive to inspire you. Otherwise, you may lose the enthusiasm that you had when you started. The solution is to find a higher aspect of the work that you love and enjoy, and dedicate your actions to it. Think of it as an altar at which you mentally offer your actions.

The first motivating factor could be the people you serve. Examples include a doctor who loves his patients, a tour guide who loves meeting people from different countries, or a mother dedicated to her family. The second factor could be the service you provide. Whether small or significant, you can have the satisfaction of knowing that the service you provide helps others in some way. You could be a

---

[7] Ibid., footnote 1, 188.

cashier at a supermarket, a policeman, a mortgage broker, or a high-ranking politician. Third, the cause that you work for can be a great motivator for you. For instance, you could be a soldier fighting to protect lives and maintain peace in your country.

Having an altar of dedication that you love makes you feel that the work itself is your reward. No task feels like a burden or inconvenience, no matter how small or routine it may be. The higher your altar of dedication, the more inspired you will be. The more the inspiration, the greater the work will bring out the best in you. As Vedantic master Swami Tejomayananda puts it, "An altar in life alters your life."[8]

The highest altar of dedication is the Supreme Consciousness or *Om*—the source from which all things and beings emerge, and which pervades them all.[9] All our actions at the body, mind, and intellect level are possible solely because of its enlivening presence. Therefore, it's apt to gratefully offer all our actions to it. Dedicating our actions to a higher altar is the essence of *karma yoga*. What's wonderful is that the attitude of dedication to this noble altar turns everyday work into worship.[10]

---

[8] Tejomayananda, *An Altar in Life, Alters Your Life*, 1.

[9] Chinmayananda, *Holy Geeta,* 18.46, 1111.

[10] Ibid., 1112.

Gurudev is my altar of dedication. Having attained the realization of the Supreme Consciousness, he is the personification of it. I keep a simple affirmation in mind as I work, and strive to live up to it: "Only you—for you." I say, "Only you" because as the enabler of my actions, I consider him to be the real doer. It's only he, and not me. And by saying "for you" I drop my expectations of the rewards of my actions and dedicate them to him.

When we dedicate our actions to a higher altar, we temporarily give up the ego that wants to claim credit for doing the actions. This helps erode our *vasanas,* which form when actions are done with an egocentric sense of agency or a feeling that "I did it."[11] It is this sense of agency that spurs us to perform actions prompted by personal likes and dislikes and crave particular results. In other words, it makes us work with attachment.

Karma yoga helps exhaust our *vasanas* instead of accumulating them.[12] As the *vasanas* decrease, the impurities decrease. This makes the mind more peaceful and balanced, which in turn gives it a greater ability to concentrate in meditation. As one progresses in meditation, the ego is eventually transcended, and the pure Self is realized.

---

[11] Ibid., 1116.

[12] Ibid., 175.

The Art of Action

The art of action is beautifully encapsulated in this verse from the *Bhagavad Gita, Thy right is to work only, but never to its fruits; let not the fruit of action be thy motive, nor let thy attachment be to inaction.*[13]

The first part of this verse, "Thy right is to work only, but never to its fruits," tells us that we can choose what actions to perform, but we have no claim or control over the types of results we get, how we get them, and when they come. The results of actions, or the "fruits," emerge from an interplay of many other factors.

Let's say you have an important presentation at work. You research, plan, and prepare for it. How it turns out, however, depends on many factors. Do you have everything you need and is it functioning properly (the projector, the screen, the slide clicker, the computer)? Is everyone who is supposed to be present there? What mood are they in? So you can put in your very best effort in preparing and presenting, but the success of your presentation depends on many factors out of your control. Can you think of a time when you put in your best effort, but things didn't turn out the way you had expected?

Understanding that the results of our actions are out of our hands, the verse continues to advise us to

---

[13] Chinmayananda, *Holy Geeta*, 2.47, 114.

do actions without being concerned about gaining specific outcomes of our efforts. "Let not the fruit of action be thy motive."

Now, you may ask why would you do anything at all if you're not motivated to gain the desired results of your actions? It's not that we shouldn't have plans and goals for our work. We are advised to not focus on the results of our actions *while* we are doing the actions. This frees up our mind to focus on the task at hand, thus increasing our efficiency and chances of success.

Lastly, the verse tells us not to let laziness stop us from doing what we should and could be doing: "nor let thy attachment be to inaction." It also means that if we think that we won't get the results that we desire from our actions, we may feel discouraged or unmotivated to do them at all. We should not avoid doing work because of our attachment to future rewards.

The Secret to Being Happy

Applying the principles of *karma yoga* to our work helps us to be happy regardless of the results we get. Let's see how this is so.

The results of actions can be of three kinds—desirable, undesirable, or mixed.[14] Desirable results

---

[14] Ibid., 18.12, 1056.

make us happy because we get what we were hoping for. Examples include receiving a good bonus at the end of the year, finding the perfect job, or being able to buy the last two tickets to see a sold-out show. Undesirable results make us unhappy because they are unwanted by us. Examples are an event that flops after months of planning, losing money in an investment, or failing an exam. Mixed results may be good in one way but not so good in another, for example, finding a suitable new house in your preferred neighborhood but it's on a busy street, receiving a good promotion that also demands that you work weekends, or eating at a restaurant that has a pleasing ambience and good service but the food isn't very tasty.

Gaining undesirable and mixed results leaves us dissatisfied and unhappy. They motivate us to continue doing more actions to find the happiness we want. But even desirable results are unsatisfactory. This is because the happiness isn't permanent and is tainted with a fear of loss or change in the desirable thing, situation, or relationship. For example, let's say you bought a lottery ticket and won five million dollars. After the initial excitement and happiness dies down, you may start to fear that with your long list of wants, you'll quickly run out of money. Or you fear that you won't manage the money well, and you begin to stress about how to maximize your winnings—what to spend them on, where to invest them, whom to give them to, and how much. Your good fortune doesn't come with peace of mind.

Think about these facts: We do actions to reap happiness from enjoying desirable future results. But the results are not always desirable. Even if they are, the happiness doesn't last and is spoiled with fear. Next, we are in control only of the actions we choose to do, and the attitude with which we do them; not the outcome. The strange thing is that instead of focusing on what we *can* control now, we've made our happiness dependent on future results that are unknown, temporary, and *out* of our control. This keeps us continuously chasing an elusive future happiness.

Why wait to be happy later? It's wiser to work without ego and attachment to the results, giving full attention to the task at hand. This quiets the chattering mind. When the mind is calm, a spring of joy that is within flows out and is channeled into the work. You may have experienced the feeling of being so happily immersed in your work that you became unaware of time and the other things that normally occupy your mind.

Detaching from the anxiety to gain the results of action by finding happiness *in the action itself* is the simple secret to being happy now. Can you think of how you can detach from worrying about a particular outcome when taking on your next task or project at home or at work?

The principles of *karma yoga* apply to everyone, young and old alike. Here they are again in brief:

- Always do your duties.
- Do them readily, cheerfully, and to the best of your ability.
- Work without attachment. This means working without ego, personal likes and dislikes, and insistence on any tangible or intangible results.
- Dedicate your actions to a higher altar, and stay focused on the work at hand.
- No matter what results you get, accept them graciously without complaint.

Working in this way will bring you happiness in your day-to-day life and efficiency in action. Importantly, it will reduce your *vasanas,* cleanse the impurities in your mind, and help you grow spiritually.

Bhakti Yoga—the Path of Devotion

Thoughts constantly flowing in love toward the Supreme is devotion.
—Swami Chinmayananda, *Discourses on Narada Bhakti Sutra*

Bhakti yoga, or the Path of Devotion, is the discipline of maintaining a steady stream of love-filled thoughts toward the supreme cause of creation or, for simplicity, I'll use "God." And when I refer to God, I'll use "Him." You can substitute that pronoun with "Her" or "It" as you feel comfortable.

The mind is easily distracted and jumps from one thing to the next, seldom staying in one place for long. In *bhakti yoga*, the mind's attention is repeatedly pulled away from the various changing worldly things, beings, and matters and placed on one constant, unchanging presence—God.[15] Because of this, *bhakti yoga* reduces the restlessness of the mind. *Bhakti yoga* also brings inner purification. This happens because the loving remembrance of God uplifts the mind and removes negative thoughts and emotions. A seeker on this path strives to cultivate an unflinching faith in and an intense longing for God.

---

[15] Chinmayananda, *Narada Bhakti Sutra,* 4.

How to Develop and Practice Devotion

Love for God does not come on its own. It has to be cultivated through some special means. All religions teach various methods, and I'd like to share what I've learned from the Hindu epic poem the *Ramayana*. The *Ramayana* tells the story of Lord Rama, who is worshipped as an embodiment of the Supreme Reality. In it, Lord Rama explains nine ways to develop divine devotion.[16] The techniques are not unique to Hinduism, and you'll probably be able to relate to them.

1. *Be in the company of noble souls.* Noble souls are people devoted to God and see that one Cause in everyone. They are great givers of love. Being in the company of such people will kindle love for God in our hearts and give rise to a desire to share that love with others.

2. *Listen to the stories of God.* All traditions and religions have stories that describe the miracles and glory of God. Listening to them elevates us, inspires us, and creates deep love and faith in God. "Listening" in today's world includes reading or watching depictions of the stories of God.

---

[16] Tulasidasa, "Aranya-kanda," in *Sri Ramacaritamanasa,* 34.4–35.1–3, 697–98.

3. *Humbly serve your true guru.* A true guru is someone who has achieved oneness with the Supreme Truth and guides others to the same goal. There are thousands of such masters from all traditions of the world. Jesus Christ, Buddha, Prophet Mohammad, Ramana Maharshi, and Swami Chinmayananda are only a few well-known examples of such great gurus and masters. Humbly serving your guru in his divine mission is serving God. Over time, such selfless service leads to a deep love for God.

4. *Sing the praises of God with no selfish motive.* True prayer is connecting with the Supreme with feelings of love and gratitude. But often we pray only when we need something. Gurudev used to joke that we don't "pray to" God, we "prey upon" God, hounding Him to fulfill our long list of wants. We strike up "deals" where we beg for a lot and promise to give back some paltry thing when our desires are fulfilled. A true devotee sings God's praises without any selfish motive. She only prays for more and more love for Him.[17] She wants nothing else.

5. *Chant the holy name of God with unwavering faith.* Chanting a name of God invokes His presence

---

[17] Chinmayananda, *Narada Bhakti Sutra,* 14.

and divinizes our thoughts. It is a great remedy for the impurities of the mind. In fact, chanting the holy name of God is "the easiest way to be freed from the worst of sins."[18] The power of God is contained in the name of God. When we chant His name with faith, the hidden power in that name manifests, destroying our sins and bringing us closer to Him.[19]

6. *Control the senses and live a clean, chaste life.* Allowing ourselves to be controlled by our senses keeps our focus on worldly pleasures, pushing our spiritual goals to the background. It also stirs up negative emotions and prompts us to take wrong actions. Living a chaste life of self-control and moderation makes it easier to grow in devotion to God.

7. *See God in All.* God is the creator of all and resides in all. At the core of all beings is this divine presence. Striving to see God in all will not only open our hearts in warm acceptance and reverence for everyone but also increase our love for the creator. A sincere devotee sees the whole world as the very form of God.[20]

---

[18] Tejomayananda, *Shrimad Bhagavata*, 353.

[19] Ibid., 358.

[20] Chinmayananda, *Narada Bhakti Sutra*, 18.

8. *Be content in life and never point out the faults of others.* In life we always get what we have earned as the results of our own past actions. We are advised to be content and not compare what we have with others. When we compare, feelings of envy and jealousy arise. These feelings separate us from others and make us want to point out others' faults. Pointing out the faults of others doesn't highlight how bad they are; rather, it reflects on the kind of people *we* are.

9. *Be honest and straightforward in your dealings with others and have firm faith in God at all times.* No one likes to be cheated or lied to. We should be open in our interactions with others, holding no underlying selfish motives. If there is full faith in God and His protection, we needn't worry about the danger of being taken advantage of by others, or fearing we will lose face, wealth, or possessions. We must have faith in the inherent goodness of God and that He always has our back.

Lord Rama tells us that even if we sincerely practice only one of the above nine means of devotion, love for the divine will take root in our hearts.

One practice that I have taken up is chanting a

holy name. There are literally thousands of names of God from all the spiritual traditions of the world. If this is a discipline that you would like to take up, you can chant a name that resonates with you. The *mantra* (sacred chant) that I have taken up is *Sri Rama Jai Rama Jai Jai Rama*. It means glory or victory to Lord Rama, who dwells in the hearts of all and gives joy to all.[21] I chant it when I sit for my daily spiritual practice and also strive to chant it mentally throughout the day.

There is a special discipline that is explained in the devotional Hindu scripture called the *Shrimad Bhagavata* that I do every day. This discipline is said to be the duty of all people everywhere, man or woman, young or old. When practiced, it brings the highest good of all.[22] Through this discipline, one attains God.[23] The practice is encapsulated in this Sanskrit prayer:

> *kaayena vaachaa manasendriyair vaa*
> *buddhyaatmanaa vaa prakriteh svabhaavaat*
> *karomi yadyat sakalam parasmai*
> *naaraayanaayeti samarpayaami*
> — *Shrimad Bhagavata,* 11.2.36[24]

It means: "Whatever I do with my body, speech,

---

[21] Tejomayananda, *Universal Questions and Timeless Answers*, 13.

[22] Tejomayananda, *Shrimad Bhagavata*, 836.

[23] Ibid., 837.

[24] Ibid., 838.

mind, sense organs or intellect and ego due to my own nature, I offer it all to the supreme Lord."[25]

God is our life-giver, sustainer, and the enabler of all our actions. The best spiritual discipline is therefore to keep Him in our minds at all times and mentally offer all our actions to Him. So whether you are working at the office or at home, walking, driving, eating, drinking, exercising—literally every action that you perform can be offered to God.[26]

In fact, not only should we offer all our actions, but the *Shrimad Bhagavata* also advises us to surrender our sense of possessiveness and concerns about our family members, wealth, and belongings, and offer them all to God. Ultimately, everything and everyone comes from God, and so we all belong to Him. He alone will take care of us. By always offering everything to God, we will slowly begin to feel that everything is indeed His alone. In this way, devotion will develop in our hearts.[27]

To be able to offer everything to God and grow in devotion, we must have a relationship with Him. The first thing to do is to set up a connection. You can begin by seeing Him (or Her) as your master, guru, father, mother, brother, sister, or a good friend. God

---

[25] To hear me chant this prayer, go to
   www.ManishaMelwani.com/prayer-of-surrender/
[26] Ibid., 839.
[27] Ibid., 870.

is infinite and can be invoked in any way that you like. Once you've determined your connection with God, building a relationship is similar to how you would build a good relationship with your friends or family members. You would cultivate it through frequent contact, heartfelt communication, and the sharing of common experiences. In other words, you would continuously reach out to God in your thoughts, talk to Him, and remember Him in all that you do. You would ask Him for guidance for your life and offer all your concerns and actions to Him. A true devotee surrenders her whole life to God.

As you bring in the remembrance of God in all aspects of your daily life, He will eventually become the center of your life, and a trustworthy confidant whom you will come to love and have faith in. All your efforts in practicing *bhakti yoga* will eventually lead you to become one with your beloved in your heart.

CHAPTER 10

The Path of Knowledge

A seeker in Vedanta is expected to carry out daring intellectual flights to the Unknown through a process of deep study, vigorous reflections and tireless meditations.

—Swami Chinmayananda,
Talks on Sankara's Vivekachoodamani

Jnana Yoga—the Path of Knowledge

Picture an exquisite diamond lying at the bottom of a lake, buried by centuries of mud and debris. Legends about its immense worth and magical qualities abound in the people living in that area. It is said that the one who finds it will achieve everlasting peace and happiness.

Like countless people before you, you also go to the lake to find out the truth of the legend. But in addition to the muddy waters, the lake is extremely turbulent. No matter how many times you dive into the water looking for the diamond, you simply can't find it. Frustrated, you begin to doubt its very existence. You tell yourself that even if it *is* there, the stories about it are all false. After all, how could the discovery of a thing make a person eternally happy? And so the priceless gem continues to remain there, waiting to be discovered.

The diamond in this little story represents your soul, and the water represents your mind. The mud in the water stands for selfish desires and negative emotions that make your mind impure. The choppy water portrays the restlessness and ever-changing thoughts of your mind. Not knowing the truth of the diamond's presence and its qualities symbolizes ignorance of your true spiritual nature.

Impurities, restlessness, and spiritual ignorance are the three inherent defects of the mind. You first read about them at the end of chapter 1. As you reduce these three defects, you'll begin to bring out the spiritual shine from within you.

Doing your duties in the *karma yoga* spirit decreases the impurities of the mind. The practice of *bhakti yoga* further cleanses the mind and makes it calm and focused. When the impurities and restlessness lessen, you'll be ready for the Path of Knowledge, or *jnana yoga,* (pronounced "nyaana yoga"). Learning Vedanta is following the Path of Knowledge. This path will provide you with an understanding of your true nature and the means to rediscover it. When you do, you'll come face-to-face with your "diamond"—your soul, your true Self.

Karma yoga and *bhakti yoga* are the preparatory disciplines that you must practice before you are suitably ready for the more demanding Path of Knowledge. Only then will you be ready to *fully understand, retain, and apply* spiritual knowledge in your life. Without the right preparation, the spiritual knowledge that you learn will remain as mere information and bring no inner transformation.

Here's an example to illustrate why the mind has to be prepared before you can get the most out of *jnana yoga*: Think of an old plate that is covered with thick layers of hard, grimy, disgusting food waste accumulated from many years of neglect. Before you can eat from it, you'll have to thoroughly clean the plate. You can begin by soaking it in warm soapy water for some time and then using a metal scraper or a hard brush to remove the old food. You can then use a sponge and some dish soap to scrub off the remaining particles of food. Finally, the plate has to be rinsed with clean water. You may have to soak, scrape, sponge, and rinse many times to get a suitably clean plate.

The dirty plate is a metaphor for the condition of our minds that are now impure and restless. Spiritual knowledge, symbolized by fresh, nourishing food, will be spoiled if it is served on a plate that is filthy and covered with stale, dried-on leftovers. To gain a sense of fullness and satisfaction from the fresh food, the plate must be thoroughly cleaned.

The goal in *jnana yoga* is transcending your identification with the not-Self (the body, mind, and intellect) and attaining oneness with the Self. If you are a thinker and are naturally introspective, this path is for you.

A seeker on this path begins her journey with many questions about life: How can I find more meaning in my life? What am I really searching for? If happiness is within me, how can I find it? Does God really exist? Where is He and why does He allow suffering? Why did He create the world in the first place?

These are questions that she asks not just out of a casual curiosity but from a genuine desire to gain the answers and make sense out of life. She actively looks for the answers in books and other channels, discussing life with like-minded people, learning through her own experiences and those of others, and then finally coming to a point in her life when she longs for a wise teacher who will show her a clear path to end all her lingering doubts and confusion.

Gurudev compares a seeker to a flower and the

guru to the bee that comes to pollinate it.[1] While the flower is in the bud stage, it exudes no fragrance and the bee is not attracted to it. But once the flower starts to mature and unfold its petals, the bee is irresistibly attracted to its bright color and scent. Similarly, while a person isn't ready or if she's not seeking spiritual guidance, a true guru doesn't find her. But when she is, the guru will surely come into her life to guide and teach her. One should never doubt this.

The guru of Vedanta then takes her under his wing and instructs her on the spiritual knowledge that she yearns for. Slowly and gradually, as her questions are answered, her mind settles down and becomes ready for subtler knowledge and practices.

"Through discriminative self-analysis and logical thinking" the guru teaches her how to separate the true Self from her body, mind, and intellect, just as one separates rice from the outer layers such as the husk and bran that are covering it.[2] The guru explains that since she is aware of the changing conditions of her body and personality, she cannot *be* them. He urges her to repeatedly ponder this and affirm, "I am never the ego, mind, intellect, and body."[3] He tells her that she is the inner witness who

---

[1] Chinmayananda, *Talks on Sankara's Vivekachudamani,* DVD, lecture 1.

[2] Chinmayananda, *Atmabodha,* verse 16, 34.

[3] Tejomayananda, *Living Vedanta,* verse 3, 12.

is "without attributes, desires, thoughts and actions. [She] is changeless, without form, ever free and immaculate."[4] He assures her that the consistent affirmation of her true nature as the Self, reinforced with deep reflection, will eliminate "[her] spiritual ignorance just as medicine destroys disease."[5]

Gurudev's quotation at the beginning of this chapter aptly sums up the daily practices of a seeker on the Path of Knowledge: The Self, which is the "Unknown" is to be realized through "a process of deep study, vigorous reflections and tireless meditations." You may find this description rather daunting. But don't let it scare you. It describes an advanced seeker. You can begin where you are right now by making some tweaks within yourself.

The Four Qualities of a Fit Seeker of Self-Knowledge

There are four inner qualities that will ensure your progress and success on the Path of Knowledge. If you don't have them, don't worry. It's good to know what they are and slowly work at developing them. I remember when I first learned the qualities of a fit student, I questioned my eligibility to join a Vedanta

---

[4] Chinmayananda, *Atmabodha,* verse 34, 68.

[5] Ibid., verse 37, 72.

study group. But I was welcomed into the group and started my studies. Keeping up with the studies, along with my practice of *karma yoga* and *bhakti yoga*, have helped me imbibe the qualities to some degree. I still have a long way to go, but I am further along than when I first started.

The four qualities are discrimination between the permanent and impermanent, dispassion, the group of six qualities, and a yearning for liberation.[6]

1. Discrimination between the permanent and impermanent

The first quality is a keen sense of discrimination or discernment. It comes when you've examined life closely and reflected deeply on the fact that all your experiences invariably end in sorrow—unwelcome changing conditions or circumstances, painful separation, a nagging sense of incompleteness, and the ever-present desire for more happiness. You long for something enduring that will fulfill you.

You learn that to be able to recognize the changes happening in and around you, there must be a changeless entity within you.[7] This is because all changes can only happen on a "changeless substratum."[8] A movie screen is a good example to

---

[6] Tejomayananda, *Tattvabodha,* 13.

[7] Chinmayananda, *Self-Unfoldment,* 33.

[8] Ibid.

explain what a changeless substratum is. The screen is unchanging and real, while the images that are projected on it are changing and unreal. Without a changeless substratum (the screen), you wouldn't be able to see and know the changing images. Similarly, without the presence of your true Self, the permanent, changeless, and real entity within you, you wouldn't be able to experience and know all the changes in your body, mind, intellect and in the outer world.

Having understood this, you look beyond the surface of things and seek out a more meaningful connection to them. Constantly observing and thinking, you pierce through the changes you're experiencing and place your attention on your Self, who is observing your varied experiences. In this way, you continuously discriminate between the permanent and the impermanent, the changeless and the changing, the real from the unreal.[9]

2. Dispassion

The second quality is dispassion. When you have discriminated well and have a good grasp of what is real and unreal, your false expectations and hopes of finding true happiness in the world fall away. A feeling of disinterest or detachment from the world

---

[9] Ibid., 184.

arises in you. Your peace of mind and holding a strong connection to your true Self is paramount. Any attachment to a thing, idea, situation, or person that agitates your mind is carefully analyzed, rectified with right thinking and right actions, and then readily dropped.

3. Group of six qualities

Next, there is a group of six qualities that are considered our inner wealth of character. Just as the beauty of the dawn precedes the rising of the sun, these six qualities beautify our character and indicate the coming of Self-knowledge.[10] They appear to be different from each other but are interdependent. The development of one promotes the development of the other five. The six qualities are:

i. *Control or mastery over your mind.*[11] When you have control over your mind, you're able to stand apart and not react, get carried away, or participate in negative thoughts. You can make your mind do what *you* want it to do.

ii. *Control of the senses.* The ears, skin, eyes, tongue, and nose are the organs that take in the sense of sound, touch, sight, taste, and smell. The spiritual masters tell us that the

---

[10] Tejomayananda, *Tattvabodha,* 19.

[11] Ibid.

senses are instruments that should be used with care and moderation. We should be able to control and use them as and when we want.

iii. *Self-withdrawal.* When you have mastery over your mind and senses, you naturally withdraw into yourself. You are not affected by the mental disturbances that come from things of the world.[12]

iv. *Forbearance.* Everyday life brings sorrows in the form of small inconveniences and annoyances. Forbearance is the capacity to silently and cheerfully endure them without complaining.[13]

v. *Faith.* This is having faith in the words of the spiritual teacher and the spiritual teachings.[14] It's being convinced of the integrity and ability of the teacher and the authenticity of the knowledge that he teaches.

vi. *Single-mindedness.* The last of the six qualities is the capacity to focus on a single task or goal. The only goal of a true seeker is the Self. To gain it, you control your mind and senses, withdraw from external distractions,

---

[12] Chinmayananda, *Self-Unfoldment,* 189.

[13] Tejomayananda, *Tattvabodha*, 24.

[14] Ibid., 26.

cheerfully bear the little pinpricks of life, and faithfully follow the path charted out by your teacher and the spiritual teachings.[15]

4. Yearning for liberation

The fourth and last quality of a seeker of Self-Knowledge is an intense yearning for liberation.[16] This is a deep and urgent desire to free yourself of all the sorrows springing from the world, once and for all. This is not to escape them but to seek out the true source of happiness—the Self. You want nothing else.

If you feel intimidated with this list of qualities, don't be. The truth is, you already have them, but perhaps not in full measure. For example, when you are buying a car or a home, or figuring out where and how to invest your money, you are using discrimination. When you drop unimportant activities to meet a deadline at work, you are exercising detachment and single-mindedness. When you choose not to complain about the weather or get annoyed with the long line at the store checkout, you are practicing forbearance. All you have to do now is to cultivate these qualities by exercising them more

---

[15] Ibid., 29.
[16] Ibid.

often and, importantly, holding the intention to do this to advance your spiritual growth.

When you do this, you will never get tired or bored of your spiritual activities. Growing spiritually will become an exciting challenge that will bring you ever-increasing satisfaction.

Three Steps to Reveal the Self

Even though you and I are essentially the Self functioning as our human personalities, we don't identify with our real nature. We consider ourselves human, not divine. This is because we are ignorant of the existence of the Self within us. All our problems, difficulties, and conflicts stem from the fact that we don't know our infinite, blissful nature. To help us regain the knowledge of the Self, Vedanta prescribes three steps: listening, reflection, and meditation.[17] The greater the presence of the four qualifications described above in us, the greater our success in carrying out these three steps and gaining a firsthand knowledge of the Self.

1. Listening

The traditional method of learning Self-knowledge was by listening to a master teach it. This is why

---

[17] Chinmayananda, *Self-Unfoldment*, 164.

"listening" is the first step to gaining that knowledge. Until a spiritual master educates us about our true nature, we are totally unaware of it. Only then do we come to know that there is a reality beyond what we are able to grasp through our senses, mind, and intellect. Listening to a spiritual master directly, or learning indirectly through spiritual writings, removes ignorance of the Self.[18] When listening to the teacher, we are asked to not merely hear the words, but listen with full attention.

2. Reflection

Gaining the knowledge through listening does not guarantee that it's understood. To ensure that we fully understand and retain what we have taken in, we must repeatedly ponder the knowledge presented by the master and the teachings. Reflection brings clarity to our understanding and deepens it.

3. Meditation

Even when we have heard and understood well, there may still be some confusion around the apparent contradiction between the new knowledge and our everyday experience. "How can *I* be infinite, free, and blissful?" you ask. This doubt is cleared in meditation. "Meditation is the process by which we

---

[18] Ibid.

make the understood truths our own."[19] It gives us a personal experience of the truth of the teacher's words that we are indeed the infinite Self.

We don't need to "produce" the Self or find it. It is always here, behind the body, mind, intellect, and ego. We can compare the Self to the sun that is shining, but not seen because it is hidden behind the clouds. The clouds can be compared to the body, mind, intellect, and ego. When the clouds move away— when we no longer identify with the four aspects—the sun that was already there reveals itself. [20]

Integrating the Three Yogas

The three yogas—*karma, bhakti,* and *jnana*—are recommended for people with different personalities. People who are action-oriented enjoy *karma yoga.* For those who are more emotional in their personality makeup, *bhakti yoga* comes naturally to them. And for the truly intellectual type, *jnana yoga* is recommended.[21] However, none of us are exclusively of one type. We are a blend of all three. So the best approach is a blended one.

---

[19] Ibid.

[20] Chinmayananda, *Atmabodha*, verse 4, 7.

[21] Chinmayananda, *Self-Unfoldment*, 110.

If you enjoy being active, you can focus on doing your actions in the *karma yoga* spirit and then lovingly dedicate the results to God. Your actions will be divinized through devotion and enhanced with a proper understanding of the right attitude with which to do them.

If you are heart oriented, you can focus on developing devotion toward God. Devotion will sweeten your spiritual studies, contemplation, and meditation, and express itself in loving, selfless service of others.

If you are an intellectual type who loves to know and learn, your spiritual studies will give you a sound understanding of the bigger picture of life, what your goal is, and how to get there. You'll do your duties with the right attitude, knowing their importance to your spiritual growth. You'll appreciate the importance of developing your heart and put in efforts to express love for others and for God.

The surest way to progress spiritually is to fully understand the principles of *karma*, *bhakti*, and *jnana yoga* and integrate them into your life.

CHAPTER 11

Meditation

It is in the seat of meditation that we learn to use the mind to rise beyond the mind—and realize the Truth as our own innermost Self.
—Swami Chinmayananda, *Self-Unfoldment*

The Messy Mind

You've seen images of tranquil women, meditating cross-legged in some quiet sanctuary. You crave for the feeling of peace that those images evoke. But when you try to meditate, hordes of unruly thoughts rise up and take away all chances of finding inner peace. In frustration, you wonder, "Why can't I meditate?"

Right now, your mind is a messy jumble of thoughts about your worries, regrets, fears, excitements, and plans. For example: "I don't know how I'll finish these reports by Friday." "I shouldn't have rushed to sign that contract." "I hope he doesn't get into trouble with those bullies at school again." "I can't wait to watch the finals of the match tonight." "I hope the weather holds up this weekend, so I can get those gardening chores done." In addition, your mind is hurt, and your ego is bruised through your interactions with people and situations during the day. For example: "Why did he say that? I wish he would've kept his mouth shut." "Why doesn't anyone listen to me?" "Who does she think she is—bossing me around like that!" . . . and so on. There isn't usually time to deal with or express these little hurts as you go about meeting the immediate demands of the day. These hurts build up as anger, anxiety, hatred, and other negative emotions. Naturally, when you sit down to meditate, all those messy thoughts and suppressed emotions come to the surface and disturb you.

We all want peace of mind—freedom from all agitations and sorrows. This is because peace and bliss is our essential nature. Our serene Self is to be rediscovered in meditation. It is not far away but present right here and now, behind the mind. Just as a river is made up of a flow of water, the mind is a flow of thoughts.[1] So long as the waters of a river are flowing, you can't see the riverbed, its substratum. Similarly, so long as the thoughts flow, you don't recognize the Self, the substratum that's

---

[1] Chinmayananda, *Self-Unfoldment,* 84.

hidden behind the thoughts. How do you get behind them?

Thoughts continually rise up and die away. There is a very tiny, silent space between the end of one thought and the rise of another. Ordinarily, the thoughts flow so swiftly that we're not aware of this space. It's like a movie where film frames are laid out serially and played at a certain speed to give the appearance of an unbroken moving scene.[2] If you are able to consciously slow down and reduce the thoughts, you can increase the space between them. The Supreme Truth, your spiritual essence, is to be realized in the space between the thoughts. Once the thoughts are quieted and you hold your attention steadily on the silent space between them, the Self that was already there reveals itself. This idea can be illustrated with a simple example: Imagine standing at a railroad crossing, waiting for a fast-moving train to come to a halt. While it's moving, you can't see the scene behind it. As it slows down, you catch glimpses of the view between the railcars. When it finally stops, and you place your attention between two railcars, you clearly see the scene beyond.

The three *yogas* outlined in chapters 9 and 10 prepare our minds for greater success in meditation. *Karma yoga* reduces the *quantity* of thoughts in the

---

[2] Chinmayananda, *Vivekachoodamani,* 104.

mind; *bhakti yoga* improves the *quality* of the thoughts by lifting them in love for the divine; and *jnana yoga* moves the *direction* of thoughts away from worldly matters and concerns and puts it on the Self, spirituality, and our spiritual growth.[3] The following two sections describe the outer and inner preparations for meditation.

Outer Preparation

1. Place

Creating a dedicated space for your meditation practice and using it regularly trains your mind to automatically become quiet when you go there. Find a place where you can be alone and undisturbed. It could be a special room in your home or just a quiet corner that is not used for anything else but for quiet reading, contemplation, and meditation.

Set up a small table as your altar. Cover it with a simple cloth or a shawl. Place a few objects on it that hold a special meaning for you. Use symbols that will help bring peace and inspiration to your mind. These could be spiritual or religious symbols that help you find a connection with nature, God, the prophets, saints, and masters. They could be in the form of photographs, figures, or any other objects.

---

[3] Chinmayananda, *Self-Unfoldment,* 110–11.

For instance, you could use a cross, an *Om*, a lotus, a statue of a goddess, or a meditating Buddha. It's also a good idea to light an oil lamp, candle, or tea light at your altar. It will provide a soothing ambience to your practice.

Place your personal journal, inspirational quotes, and spiritual books in your sacred space. Make sure that there aren't too many objects on your altar as they can be distracting. You want to keep your sacred space simple, clean, and uncluttered so as to bring an easy peace to your mind. My meditation space is a small walk-in closet that's about four feet wide. There is a shelf with two drawers underneath to store my books and journal.

2. Seat

Your meditation seat can be on the floor or on a chair. Use a seat that is not too soft or too hard—firm yet comfortable.[4] If you're sitting on the floor, you can make up your own seat using a folded blanket or shawl, or a low cushion. Use a seat made up of natural fibers such as wool or cotton, as they provide the most comfort. If you need a support for your back, use an armless chair and place a small blanket or shawl on the seat. An armless chair will allow you to either cross your legs or place your feet

---

[4] Chinmayananda, *Holy Geeta,* 6.11, 368.

on the floor. Chairs with arms don't allow you to easily cross your legs, and they may also raise your shoulders if the arms are not the right height for you. This may strain your neck and shoulders. You want to keep your body as relaxed as possible.

3. Posture

If you would like to sit on the floor, cross your legs, place your hands palms up in your lap, with your right palm over your left.[5] If you're using a chair, cross your legs, relax your shoulders, and place your hands in the same way as above. If you choose not to cross your legs, keep both feet flat on the floor. Make sure that you don't lean back into your chair. You can use a cushion to support your lower back.

To stay alert, the mind has to be supported by a proper upright posture. Hold your body firm and steady with your head, neck, and back in a straight line.[6] Try not to move even an inch. Make sure that you don't strain any muscles but stay as relaxed as you can. When you keep your body still, your mind gradually becomes still.[7]

Hold this posture for the entire time you are doing your practice. Gurudev used to joke that

---

[5] Chinmayananda, *Meditation and Life,* 117.

[6] Chinmayananda, *Holy Geeta,* 6.13, 372.

[7] Chinmayananda, *Art of Contemplation,* 6.

we start off as exclamation marks and end up as question marks!

4. Sense organs

Withdraw your five sense organs from their usual fields of perceptions.[8] Pay no attention to smells entering the nose, sounds heard by the ears, and textures felt by the skin. Don't engage your sense of taste by eating or chewing anything. Lastly, shut out the forms and colors of the outer world by gently closing your eyes.

Now, in a relaxed manner and with your eyes closed, turn your inner gaze to the tip of your nose.[9] By giving the eyes a focus of attention, the mind becomes focused. This is because the mind goes to where the eyes are.[10]

5. Time

The spiritual masters of Vedanta tell us that the predawn hours are the best time to practice meditation. They recommend that we wake up between four thirty and six.[11] Spiritual practices done at this time yield the best results because there is a stillness and purity in the atmosphere that allows

---

[8] Chinmayananda, *Holy Geeta*, 6.12, 370.

[9] Ibid., 6.13, 372.

[10] Ibid., 373.

[11] Chinmayananda, *Meditation and Life,* 126.

the mind to be easily impressed with positive ideas and habits.[12] If you've gone to bed early enough and are well rested, you will notice that your mind is quietly alert at this time.

As you can imagine, waking up this early isn't easy. So instead of implementing a sudden and drastic change in your routine, you can start by going to sleep thirty minutes earlier than your usual bedtime. That way, you can wake up thirty minutes earlier to sit for your meditation practice. Then, try pushing back your bedtime by fifteen-minute increments every few months until you establish an early bedtime routine. By making the changes gradually, you will increase your chances of maintaining your new routine.

Make it a habit to put meditation first. Have your morning cup of tea or coffee, or breakfast, later. You certainly don't want to check your cell phone or catch up on the latest news before sitting down for meditation. You also don't want to fit your session in just before preparing to leave for work. Your mind won't be relaxed. Give yourself enough time for the mental space you need for your spiritual practice.

Although early morning is the preferred time for meditation, you may find that your work and other duties don't allow this. So, find a time during the day

---

[12] Ibid., 130.

when you are not usually tired, and things are quiet around you. Once you find this time, don't change it. Make it your regular time for meditation.

Inner Preparation

Gurudev explains that meditation is a noun and not a verb because it is a specific state of the mind.[13] Once the mind is prepared through the correct outer and inner preparations, it becomes still and quiet. When this inner tranquility is maintained for the right amount of time, you naturally glide into a meditative state.

He compared preparing for meditation to getting ready to go to sleep.[14] When it's almost your bedtime, you put aside what you are doing, shut off the TV or computer, change into your pajamas, wash up, brush your teeth, get into bed, and then turn off the lights. These actions can be compared to the outer preparations for meditation such as coming to your sacred space, preparing your seat, lighting a lamp, sitting in the right posture, and closing your eyes.

Equally important to the outer preparations for

---

[13] Chinmayananda, *Art of Contemplation,* 9.

[14] Ibid., 4–5. The following descriptions that draw an analogy between the inner and outer preparations for sleep and the preparations for meditation are based on Swami Chinmayananda's description in *Art of Contemplation.*

sleep is the inner preparation. You have to mentally withdraw from all your concerns and hold only one thought—"I want to sleep." Then, even if you remember something you have to do or if the phone rings, you push everything aside. Your one desire for sleep overwhelms all your other desires and concerns. Holding on to it, you naturally fall asleep. It's the same inner process for getting into meditation: You turn your mind's attention away from the outer world, your body, mind, and intellect, and place it on the Self. You hold only one thought—the desire to know the Self. Maintaining the inner stillness, you naturally slip into meditation. Meditation is an effortless awareness of your true nature.[15]

Just as trying to sleep is not called "sleeping," all your efforts at getting to this peaceful abidance in the Self are not called "meditation."[16] Effort is applied to get to this state. But once there, no more effort is required. Remembering this will help you understand the difference between consciously maintaining a peaceful state of mind and spontaneously moving into meditation. Gurudev describes the state of meditation as a "new dimension of consciousness."[17] It's a higher state of consciousness that is different

---

[15] Tejomayananda, *Amrtabindu Upanishad*, 24.
[16] Chinmayananda, *Art of Contemplation*, 9.
[17] Ibid.

from the waking, dream, and deep sleep states that you go through every day.

Here are some ways to mentally prepare yourself for the shift of consciousness into the meditative state.

1. Put aside all concerns

Resolve with determination to not allow your mind to be distracted by any concerns associated with the roles that you play in your life—as daughter, son, mother, father, employer, employee, householder, business owner, community volunteer, and so on. While on the seat of meditation, mentally renounce all these roles and see yourself only as a seeker of peace, the Self or Supreme Truth.[18]

2. Be serious about your practice

Tell yourself that you will not open your eyes, move even a little, touch anything or respond to any outer sounds or smells. "I will not move or allow anything to distract me no matter what. My meditation practice is more important than any other task right now."[19]

---

[18] Tejomayananda, *Meditation*, A Vision, 21.

[19] Tejomayananda, *Bhagavad Gita Course*, lesson 10, 15.

3. Have no anxiety for any specific gains[20]

Don't have expectations of experiencing anything extraordinary such as seeing lights, hearing sounds, or gaining any psychic abilities. These expectations distract and agitate your mind.[21] Although advanced meditators do experience these things, it's important to remember that they are only *by-products* of your meditation practice and not the *real* goal of meditation. The Self is the real gain and goal. Just let go and simply "be."

4. Keep your mind calm[22]

You can do this by the preceding three points, keeping the body absolutely still and observing your breath.

5. Contemplate on a symbol of the divine[23]

Gaze at your spiritual or religious symbol and humbly invoke its grace and blessings so that you may be able to check the wanderings of your restless and unsteady mind.

---

[20] Chinmayananda, *Holy Geeta*, 6.10, 366.
[21] Tejomayananda, *Bhagavad Gita Course*, lesson 10, 13.
[22] Chinmayananda, *Holy Geeta*, 6.14, 373.
[23] Chinmayananda, *Self-Unfoldment*, 204.

The Process of Meditation

You are now ready to begin your meditation practice.

1. Go to your sacred space, sit down, and light a lamp or a candle.

2. Look at the divine symbol on your altar and turn your attention to whom or what it represents. Seek the blessings of your chosen form and dedicate your practice to it. For example, you could pray, "Dear _____, I seek your grace and blessings for my meditation practice. I dedicate my efforts to you."

3. Hold your head, neck, and back in a straight line. Place your hands in your lap and slowly close your eyes.

4. Mentally give up all your roles and concerns and see yourself solely as a seeker of peace or truth.

5. Resolve that you will keep your body very still and not allow anything to distract your attention. Tell yourself that there is nothing more important right now than your daily appointment with your Self.

6. Keep your mind calm and free from any expectations.

7. Withdraw your attention from all sense perceptions. Gently turn your inner gaze to

the tip of your nose without straining your eyes in any way.

8. Bring your attention to your breathing. Simply notice the breath; don't change it. Be aware of the cool air entering your nostrils and the warm air leaving as you exhale.

9. Now consciously slow down your breathing. Breathe in deeply. Hold the breath in momentarily, and then slowly exhale. After you exhale, hold the breath out momentarily before inhaling again. Maintain this slow, deep breathing throughout your practice.

10. Next is a technique Gurudev calls "Thought massage."[24] It involves releasing muscular tension using your thoughts. It's similar to how you would relax your muscles while lying down in the corpse pose at the end of a yoga class. Slowly visualize your body starting with your head, and gradually move down to your toes. Consciously bring your attention to each area and relax the muscles: Head, forehead, eyes, cheeks, mouth, and jaw. Neck, shoulders, upper arms, forearms, and hands. Chest and abdomen. Upper back, midback, lower back, hips, thighs, lower legs, and feet. After you've done this, your whole

---

[24] Ibid., 200.

body will feel relaxed. This technique will help to eliminate any mental agitation that could arise because of discomfort in any area of your body.

11. As you relax your body, you will notice that your mind is much quieter. When this happens, there is a tendency to verbalize the experience—"Oh wow, my mind is so quiet," "This feels good," or "I love this silence."[25] These types of thoughts will disturb the peace that you have just created. Stay silent.

12. Now that you have made your mind relatively quiet through all the previous steps, you will notice that thoughts not initiated by you will rise up. When this happens, don't get alarmed or annoyed that your peace has been disturbed. Stay calm. Don't rush to muzzle the thoughts. Focus on keeping your body and breath steady. Let the thoughts come up and die away on their own without engaging with them. Simply watch this "thought parade."[26] It would be as if you were standing on your balcony watching the traffic passing by below. This technique will calm down all

---

[25] Chinmayananda, *Art of Contemplation,* 12.

[26] Chinmayananda, *Self-Unfoldment,* 201.

remaining thought disturbances and make your mind peaceful.

13. At this point, mentally repeat a chant. You can chant a mantra or a divine name from any faith. For instance, you could chant *Om* or *Amen*. Or if you prefer, you could use words such as *peace, relax,* or *release.* Synchronize your chosen word with your breathing. For example, if you are using "Om," breathe in and say "O . . ."; breathe out and say "mmm." Use the other words in the same way: "A-men," "pe-eace," "re-lax," and "re-lease." Gradually increase the space between the chants. Finally, taper off the mental chanting so there is only silence. In silence you identify with your Self. Your goal is to focus your attention on the silence and keep it there as long as you can. Remember not to strain or force your mind to hold the silence longer than it comfortably can. Forcing it can create suppressions that will hamper your spiritual growth.[27] The silence will increase as you practice, until staying there will become effortless. This is when you will "be" in meditation.

14. When thoughts come up, begin the slow mental chanting again to divert your attention

---

[27] Ibid., 202.

from them. The thoughts will subside on their own if you don't entertain them. Keep repeating this practice until you begin to tire.

15. When you are ready to end your practice, gently bring your attention back to your body. Slowly stretch out your legs and arms, move your body, and open your eyes.

Duration and Frequency

Duration

You don't have to commit to meditating for long periods of time. Tell your mind that it has to be still for only a few minutes. Your mind is more willing to cooperate with you if it knows its commitment is only for a short time. When you first start your meditation practice, you can sit down for about five to ten minutes. You can then gradually build up your practice to about thirty minutes per day. Your goal is not to lengthen the time of your practice but to increase "the depth of silence in the mind."[28]

A word of caution: Meditation is an advanced spiritual practice. Enduring success comes very slowly and gradually over many months and even years. It's not a good idea to rush into it and sit for long periods of time simply because you enjoy the

---

[28] Chinmayananda, *Art of Contemplation*, 13.

peace that comes with it. If your mind is not prepared through the disciplines of *karma, bhakti,* and *jnana yoga,* meditation can bring up many suppressed emotions and memories that you're not ready to handle. This can make you depressed, angry, or overwhelmed. You may give up your practice altogether. So, make sure to support your meditation practice with the other three *yogas.* Also, always invoke divine grace with genuine feelings of devotion and surrender at the start of your practice. Following these important tips will make certain that your spiritual progress is steady and sure.

Frequency

Resolve to sit for meditation daily. If you can't manage this, then start with just the weekends, then three times a week, then five times, and finally, every day. If you miss a day, make sure you get right back to your routine the following day. Be businesslike about your commitment to your daily practice. Arrange your schedule around this important discipline. Regularity is the key to your success.

The Rewards

Don't let the difficulty in quieting your mind discourage you or make you give up. Consciously taking the mind away from its usual concerns even for a few minutes can help recharge and revitalize it.[29] There are many rewards along the way . . .

Your attempts to distance yourself from your thoughts will bring you a greater poise in life. Things that used to bother you won't disturb you as much. It'll become easier to let things go and move on. Even if something does shake you up, you'll have a better ability to bounce back. You won't stay down and depressed for days or weeks like you may have before.

Conflicts within your own mind will taper off as you gain more clarity and ability to stay centered on your values and priorities. Positive qualities that lie within you will begin to blossom. Your concentration will be enhanced, and with that, a greater ability to focus on achieving your everyday goals. You'll depend less on things, circumstances, and people for your sense of well-being. And therefore, you'll become happier and more peaceful in life.

Having a sincere desire to calm your mind is to be commended. The mind is a subtle inner instrument and much harder to control than the body. When you take on a sincere and regular practice of calming the mind, you are surely on the right path. In fact, there are no real pitfalls. Every attempt brings you closer to unfolding the beauty of your divine essence.

---

[29] Chinmayananda, *Self-Unfoldment,* 205.

CHAPTER 12

Daily Habits of a Spiritual Seeker

At the root of all gain is self-effort. Devote your days and nights to spiritual exercises. You will be, in the end, crowned with success.

—Swami Tapovanam,
Guidance from the Guru

Taking time out for our spiritual growth often becomes a low priority amid the busyness of daily life. Since inner growth cannot be tangibly measured, or the results immediately seen, we tend to allow everyday activities and concerns to crowd out the highly important time for our spiritual pursuits.

Growing spiritually takes time, focus, and sincere effort and doesn't happen quickly. Gurudev used to say that it is a slow evolution, and not a revolution. We have to give it priority and infuse our entire life with a spiritual view. Commitment, sincere self-application, patience, and self-discipline are vital.

> Spiritual students must develop a new relationship to the body and its worldly enjoyments. The right attitude would be to play about in the world as in a field of sport and to consider secular activities as hobbies—all the while maintaining a constant vision of the ultimate goal of human existence, that is, realization of one's true Self.[1]

This is powerful advice coming from a spiritual master who achieved Self-realization. Just think, Gurudev is asking us to live in the spirit of sportsmanship. To me, this means that we must stay positive, respect others and their rights, put in our best in all that we do, and detach from the outcome of our actions. We must also courageously meet the gains and losses, successes and failures, pleasures and pains of the game of life with an even mind. He asks us to treat our worldly activities as *hobbies* while holding the goal of achieving Self-realization constantly at the back of our minds. This is the *real work* we are here to accomplish.

Where do we begin? What are the daily practices and habits of a spiritual seeker?

---

[1] Chinmayananda, *Self-Unfoldment*, 187–88.

Spiritual Practices

Waking Up Early

As mentioned in the last chapter, the masters of Vedanta advise us to do our spiritual practice between four thirty and six in the morning. This is the time when the atmosphere is conducive to meditation. In the story of Dheera in chapter 6, I brought out this fact by writing that he attained Self-realization in the predawn hours.

I would like to share with you my personal experience relating to the daily habit of waking up early to do my reading, reflection, prayer, and meditation. If there is only one practice that you incorporate into your life after reading this book, I hope it's this one. It has been the single most transformational habit of my life.

I go to bed around ten in the evening so that I can wake up at four in the morning. Once I open my eyes, I don't hit the snooze button on my clock or allow myself to toss in bed, deciding whether or not to get up. I simply get out of bed. My inspiration is Gurudev. He says, "Don't wait for your sleep to leave you. When you wake up, get up. If you wait in your bed, you will fall asleep again. Get up, and then fully wake up."[2]

---

[2] Chinmayananda, *Art of Contemplation*, 24.

After I get up, I brush my teeth, take a shower, and so forth. This refreshes my body and mind. I put on a clean pair of pajamas that I have set out the night before. I then go to my sacred space to read from one of my Vedanta texts, reflect on what I have read, pray, and sit for meditation. I find that my mind readily absorbs what I am reading, and because it is so quiet around me, I am better able to focus in meditation.

From the time I wake up until I end my meditation practice, I am up for about an hour and a half or sometimes two. Then, because I'm tired and it's still early, I go back to sleep for about an hour until it's time for me to start the usual activities of the day. My mind is peaceful, and so my sleep is especially deep and restful. I love my early morning sleep!

The reason I say that waking up early has been the most transformational habit of my life is that to go to sleep early and wake up early, I've had to revamp my entire life. I'm more careful about choosing how I spend my day and have given up unimportant and unnecessary activities that don't fit in with my new routine. I'm especially mindful about what I do in the evening. I avoid watching TV and going on my computer late at night. I've adopted a simpler lifestyle and healthier eating habits. I'm vegetarian and I don't drink alcohol. Lighter vegetarian meals give me more energy so I don't need as much sleep at night. Heavy nonvegetarian foods, and foods high in carbohydrates, fat, and sugar, tend to drain your energy.

All these changes have taken me many years, and even now, I can't honestly say that I wake up at four every single day. My routine is frequently disturbed because of changes in my duties and commitments in my work and at home. Sometimes I can't get up early because I've been unwell, I've had a particularly tiring day, an occasional late night, or my body simply needs more sleep. Also, whenever I'm traveling, it's very difficult to stick to a routine. When I first started, I would easily lose focus or get lazy and stay up late for one reason or another. (To be honest, this still happens from time to time.)

I think all these inconsistencies are pretty normal and okay. There will invariably be some challenges when trying to establish a new habit; especially one that requires you to rework many aspects of your day. I try my best to not miss a day, but when I do, I try to make sure I don't miss more than two straight days. And if I can't wake up by four, I try to be up by six at the latest. As Gurudev puts it, "*We must*—reserve a definite time, preferably at dawn, for meditation and prayer."[3]

---

[3] Chinmayananda, *We Must*, 5.

Despite the difficulties and the self-discipline that's required, I've come to not see it as a sacrifice or inconvenience. Once I made a commitment to my new routine, the activities and people that didn't fit in fell away quite naturally. The joy and peace that I gain from my spiritual practice surpasses the short-lived joys that I used to enjoy. There really *is* a very different energy early in the morning.

What do you think? Would you like to try waking up early to do your spiritual practice? Here are some more benefits.

1. Better sleep: When you stay up late to work, read, watch TV, surf the internet, check your messages on your smartphone or tablet and engage on social media, chances are that you'll go to bed right after because you're too tired to do anything else. What you've just engaged in will leave fresh impressions in your mind that may prevent you from falling asleep easily. Or if you do fall asleep right away, they can create unpleasant dreams that may disturb your sleep. Either way, you'll get less sound sleep.

2. Better health and energy for your life: Better sleep will do this.

3. Better productivity and time management: When you have to sleep early and wake up early, you'll readily give up extraneous activities that take up precious time and don't add value to your day. You'll naturally become more productive.

4. Greater self-awareness and inner transformation: The serene early morning time spent in solitude promotes self-discovery. This will lead you to a greater awareness of the areas where you need to make positive changes in your life, behavior, and relationships.

5. A quieter, more balanced mind: As you simplify your life to fit your new schedule, you'll create mental space and quietude that will give you clarity and strength to meet your daily challenges.

6. Increased creativity: Your quiet mind will make it easier for you to tap into your intuition and find creative solutions and ideas for your life.

7. Practice in self-discipline: Adopting this habit will help you develop self-discipline, a vital character trait that can help you in other areas of your life. No worthwhile goal can be achieved without self-discipline.

As you can see, there is much wisdom in the old saying popularized by Benjamin Franklin—*Early to bed, early to rise, makes a man, healthy, wealthy and wise.*

If you're open to adopting this new habit of sleeping early and waking up early, there are three important details that I'd like to share with you.

First, make it a habit to take your mind to something spiritual and uplifting just before you go to sleep—a book or a recording. I have found that this infuses my mind with positive impressions that enable me to fall asleep easily and stay asleep. I've done it for so many years that I can't fall asleep without reading a page or two from one of my Vedanta books.

Second, take a shower and put on a clean set of clothes before going to your meditation space. I do this even in the winter. There's nothing like a shower to brighten you up and prepare you for your meditation practice. It gives it a sense of importance and surrounds you with a subtle aura of sanctity.

And third, dedicate your practice to a revered higher altar such as a realized master, saint, or God. This will inspire you and make the sacrifice and discipline easier. Without an inspiring altar, you can go for years procrastinating your start, or be unable to sustain it for long.

Going to sleep early and waking up early to read,

reflect, pray, and meditate will greatly advance your spiritual evolution. I hope you'll try it and experience the benefits yourself.

Introspection

Introspect daily as outlined in chapter 8. In addition to examining your actions and motives behind them, ask yourself if you chose the Path of the Good over the Path of the Pleasant when meeting your day.

It's also a good idea to examine how well you did in cultivating the six inner qualities of a spiritual seeker (see chapter 10). For instance, were you able to rein in your runaway thoughts and senses? Did you withdraw from distractions and stay single-minded in meeting the goals of your day? How well did you endure little obstacles that intruded unexpectedly into your plans? Did you assert your faith in the divine in your activities and interactions with others?

Self-Study and Reflection

Spiritual self-study is a must for all serious spiritual seekers. When you miss even a few days, you are prone to forget what you've learned. Don't be surprised to find that the hours you spent studying or listening to something totally disappears from your mind the next time you pick it up. Spiritual knowledge tends to evaporate very quickly because of the impurities in the mind. (Recall the story in chapter 8, of the mind being like a newspaper.) To embed the spiritual ideas into your understanding, it's important to keep up your spiritual studies *every day*.

The best sources for spiritual knowledge are authentic spiritual texts and spiritual masters who have personally lived and realized the knowledge within those texts. You can find spiritual knowledge in all the wisdom traditions of the world, including Vedanta.

It's important to note the difference between *satsang* and self-study. *Satsang* is being in spiritual company (see chapter 8). But self-study is a purposeful and serious attempt to learn and bring those ideas into your own understanding. You may find it useful to record your reflections in a notebook or on your computer. This will help you organize your thoughts and deepen your understanding. It also becomes a handy reference when you need to recall facts. Put aside fifteen to thirty minutes for spiritual studies and reflection daily.

Meditation

The goal, preparations, technique, and benefits of meditation have all been described in detail in the last chapter. Here are a few additional tips: If you're new to meditation, you can start by practicing to sit still in an upright posture, closing your eyes and being aware of your normal breathing. Practice sitting still in this way for a week. Then, you can add deep breathing to your practice, making sure to fill your entire lungs. Hold the breath in for a second or two after you breathe in, exhale, and hold the breath out for another one or two seconds. These two small pauses after you breathe in and breathe out suspend your thoughts and give you a little taste of the longer silence that you are aspiring to achieve. Don't rush. Take as much time as you need to be comfortable breathing in this way. Once you have mastered this technique, take your attention off the breathing and place it on enjoying the silence within.

When chanting a mantra, a divine name or a one-word affirmation, start with chanting out loud and then gradually lower the volume of your chanting until it becomes a soft whisper. Then take your slow chanting to the mental level.[4] When you're able to chant mentally, you're ready to follow the entire fifteen-step process described in chapter 11.

Meditation takes work and a great deal of preparation. You can't be rushing around and expect your mind to calm down as soon as you sit for meditation.

---

[4] Tejomayananda, *Upadesa Sara*, verse 6, 21.

> Let us remember that the mental attitude of meditation is not invoked by a mechanical readjustment gained in haste during an evening's "half-an-hour." [The] meditative mood is to be zealously worked for and earned by each seeker during the entire day's activities. Unless we discriminate and intelligently live almost all the twenty-three-and-a-half hours of the day, we cannot expect even half-an-hour's meditative mood.[5]

So if you are serious about meditation, you'll have to organize your day and your mind around your meditation practice. Only then will you have a mental atmosphere that's conducive for it.

A Spiritual Flavor to All Your Activities

You practice *jnana yoga* when you do your daily spiritual studies, reflection, and meditation. But these spiritual practices are only done at certain times of the day. You can add a spiritual flavor to your entire day by doing your activities in the *karma yoga* spirit and surrendering them all in devotion to the higher power.

What's wonderful about following the principles of *karma yoga* and *bhakti yoga* is that you become

---

[5] Chinmayananda, *We Must,* 36.

efficient in your work, get it done in a positive state of mind, *and* promote your spiritual growth at the same time! In the past, you may have felt that you were being pulled in different directions as you struggled to meet the various demands of work and the people around you. Your life was segmented, and your energies were dissipated into different channels. But now, your energies are streamlined and dedicated to only one altar. Your mind becomes cheerful and your interactions, naturally harmonious.

Hasten Slowly

Growing spiritually is hard work. But it's well worth the time and energy because the inner gains far outweigh any outer successes and material gains. We shouldn't however, jump in without thinking or overdo things in a newfound enthusiasm to grow. As we mature, it's important to remember that it's a journey in which we are embracing new habits and expanding our consciousness. And so, we're dealing with our own mind.

Gurudev cautioned that the mind is extremely delicate, far more delicate than a flower bud. To force or rush it to grow before it is ready would permanently impair its natural maturing.[6] "Hasten

---

[6] Chinmayananda, *Holy Geeta,* 775.

slowly" was his advice.[7] "Hasten," so that we feel the urgency and put in consistent efforts, and "slowly," to ensure we are careful in our approach.

Let's all hasten slowly on the journey toward rediscovering the infinite bliss of our own true Self. It's our spiritual destiny. We will all get there— sooner or later. I'll leave you with Gurudev's words: *Never give up. Strive on. Regularity and sincerity will take you to your goal. Spiritual unfoldment is reserved for the wise heroes.*[8]

---

[7] Chinmayananda, *Meditation and Life,* 129.

[8] Chinmayananda, *Self-Unfoldment,* 210.

Want some additional tools to help you
implement this new learning into your life?
Download your free copy of:

The Now What Workbook

www.ManishaMelwani.com/the-now-what-workbook/

APPENDIX

BIOGRAPHY
OF SWAMI CHINMAYANANDA

Swami Chinmayananda lived from May 8, 1916, to August 3, 1993. His transformation from Balakrishnan Menon, a religious rebel and skeptic, to Swami Chinmayananda, the spiritual giant, is indeed extraordinary.

Balan, as he was called in his younger days, was an extremely intelligent and naturally inquisitive child. He was raised in a loving and religious Hindu family in Kerala, South India. But he doubted the very existence of God. Self-assured and vocal, he repeatedly questioned his elders on the reasoning and logic behind the old customs and traditions that they practiced. He had no interest in following religious rituals or going to the temple and even poked fun at those who did. He was daring, outgoing, and popular with his friends.

He studied under the British education system and graduated with degrees in literature and law from Lucknow University. As a university student, he joined in the fight for India's independence from British rule, giving speeches and distributing flyers, boldly inciting people to stand up against the foreign rulers. The British came to know of his activities and imprisoned him. After India gained her freedom, he became a journalist and the subeditor of the *National Herald* newspaper in Delhi. Then known as Menon, he gained a reputation for being a controversial writer, willing to speak up about India's social and political problems.

Menon wondered about the sages who lived in the Himalayan regions. If they were enlightened, why were they not in the cities, helping to alleviate the suffering of people who lived there? The fact that most people revered them was baffling. One day, he decided to visit them and write about "how they are keeping up the bluff among the masses!"

He journeyed to the ashram (spiritual center or retreat) of Swami Sivananda in Rishikesh at the foothills of the Himalayas. Confidently, he thought he would easily expose the ineffectual lifestyle of the swami and planned on staying only two days. But once there, he was completely awestruck by Swami Sivananda's dynamic character and tireless service. He ended up staying for a whole month.

Swami Sivananda was a medical doctor before becoming a monk. In Rishikesh, he established and administered a free hospital and pharmacy. Humble and caring with boundless energy and enthusiasm, he spent all his time focused on the needs and upliftment of others. His daily routine included teaching formal classes in Vedanta for the neophytes and swamis, corresponding with spiritual seekers all around the world, receiving visitors to the ashram and patiently answering their questions, writing spiritual books and articles, and conducting devotional chanting sessions for swamis and visitors alike.

Menon returned to the ashram many times in the next two years, basking in the inspiring presence of Swami Sivananda and fully immersing himself in the daily activities. In a decision that took his family and friends by surprise, he announced that he would give up his worldly lifestyle and become a monk. In

February 1949, Balakrishnan Menon was initiated into monkhood by Swami Sivananda and gained the name Swami Chinmayananda. *Chinmaya* means "True Knowledge" in Sanskrit.

His exceptionally brilliant mind and intense desire to seek out the goal of human existence led Swami Sivananda to think that it would be better that Swami Chinmayananda left the busy ashram and spent his entire time pursuing his spiritual studies. Swami Sivananda recommended that he study under the tutelage of the great master of Vedanta, Swami Tapovanam, who lived higher up in the Himalayan mountains.

Under Swami Tapovanam, Swami Chinmayananda totally immersed himself in his spiritual studies and a life of meditation. While the lessons were in Sanskrit, the language of the ancient spiritual texts, Swami Chinmayananda wrote out his notes in English. In the tranquility of the great Himalayan mountains, Swami Chinmayananda gained spiritual enlightenment.

In December 1951, Swami Chinmayananda came down to the plains to teach spirituality. Traditionally, the spiritual texts were taught in Sanskrit, and only to the male members of the priest class. Never one to toe the line, Swami Chinmayananda's approach was startlingly different. He taught freely and openly to men and women alike without any class distinctions—and in English!

An enthusiastic and animated speaker, he conveyed ancient truths with breathtaking clarity and a modern style. He sprinkled his talks with humor and insightful examples from everyday life. People were spellbound by his brilliant and inspiring oratory. He was astonishingly popular. Indoor venues soon became too small to hold the crowds that came to listen to him. His talks took place in open public grounds that could accommodate thousands of people.

Swami Chinmayananda was an outstanding teacher who encouraged his listeners to question tradition and challenge long-standing religious dogma. He advised them to accept neither scriptural writings nor the words of spiritual masters on blind faith. He insisted that they verified the ideas that he spoke about through their personal reflection and experience before accepting them.

In 1953 a small group of enthusiastic followers in Chennai, South India, formed the Chinmaya Mission to formalize and organize the work of Swami Chinmayananda. Under his grand vision and dedication, the Chinmaya Mission grew by leaps and bounds. Today, there are more than three hundred Chinmaya Mission Centers in India and abroad, reaching out to hundreds of thousands of children, youth, and adults.

Swami Chinmayananda traveled extensively in India and around the world, staying only a few days in each place before moving on. He worked grueling eighteen-hour days, never taking any holidays. In the nights, he would often be seen writing letters to his devotees as early as three a.m.

Swami Chinmayananda, or Gurudev, as he is lovingly called, had a tenacious memory and an uncanny ability to remember names, addresses, people, and events accurately for decades afterward. There are reports of people whom he recognized and called out by name nearly thirty years later. One Californian devotee remembers talking to Gurudev in a car while driving him to the airport. Their conversation was interrupted when they arrived at their destination. They were not able to speak again until Gurudev's next trip the following year. When they met, Gurudev calmly picked up the conversation as though they had just been speaking. "So, as I was saying . . ." This is mind boggling when one considers that he met thousands of people every year.

Gurudev worked tirelessly for forty-two years right up to his last few days. He passed in San Diego, California, at the age of seventy-seven. His body was taken back to India to be buried in the lotus (cross-legged) position in his ashram in Sidhbari. Sidhbari is a little village at the foothills of the Himalayan Dhauladhar mountain range in the state of Himachal Pradesh. In accordance with Hindu custom, an enlightened master's body is allowed burial. The bodies of ordinary Hindus are cremated.

Swami Chinmayananda wrote many books and exhaustive English commentaries on traditional Vedanta texts including the *Bhagavad Gita* and *Upanishads*. The teaching of Vedanta was and always has been the main focus of the Chinmaya Mission. However, it doesn't stop there. The work of Chinmaya Mission includes a wide range of cultural, educational, community, and social service projects.

The outer expressions of Swami Chinmayananda's extensive work are only a minuscule part of the immeasurable impact that he has had on the inner transformation of thousands of people. His life was the highest expression of loving devotion to the one divine essence that he saw in all.

HOW I MET MY GURU, SWAMI CHINMAYANANDA

When we come to deserve a master, he shall reach us.

—Swami Chinmayananda,
Guru: The Guiding Light

I had a very happy childhood and family life growing up in Singapore. I am the last of three children. I had a loving mother and a jovial, fun-loving father whom I adored. In my childhood, my mother instilled in me a strong faith in God through many stories from Hindu folklore. Yet I never saw God only through the eyes of a Hindu. I went to St. Hilda's School, an Anglican mission school where we chanted the Lord's prayer and sang hymns every day. My friends were Chinese, Malay, and Indian, and came from different faiths. I loved reading inspirational and motivational books. One of my favorites was *The Power of Positive Thinking* by an American pastor, Dr. Norman Vincent Peale.

As a teenager, I developed a keen interest in sun sign astrology. I had fun getting a better understanding of people by reading the characteristics of the zodiac signs they belonged to. I enjoyed learning about palmistry, numerology, face-reading, and body language. I also had a fascination for the paranormal and for fortune-telling.

All was going well in my life until my father developed a heart condition. Then, just one month before he would have turned fifty-five, he suffered a massive heart attack and left us all too suddenly. I was twenty years old. My family and I were devastated. My mother was left like a bird with only one wing.

He had been admitted to the hospital a couple of days before, for heart-related concerns. He had the fatal attack in the early hours of the morning of the third day. Since the doctors were present at the time of his death, the paperwork was done quickly and there was no delay in releasing the body from the hospital. As per Hindu custom, it was brought back home for the final rites. The cremation was scheduled for the afternoon of the very same day. Consequently, no efforts were made to embalm the body, or pretty it up.

I remember, all too clearly, how the body was brought on a stretcher and unceremoniously dropped onto a white sheet on the cold terrazzo floor, in the middle of our living room. I looked on in horror at the body. It had no resemblance to the happy, smiling father I loved. In the few hours since his passing, it had bloated up severely, and now, bodily fluids were slowly oozing out of the eyes, nose, and mouth. I was disgusted. I remember thinking to myself, "Take that detestable thing out of the house!" I felt absolutely no connection with the ugly body lying on the floor. I didn't cry at all. I was numb with shock and disbelief.

In the days and months afterward, I struggled to make sense of his death. I had so many questions! Where had my father gone? Why did he die so young? Is there life after death? What happens when we die? Do we live many lives? What is the journey of the soul? Sun signs, fortune-telling, palmistry, and the other subjects that had interested me seemed so stupid and pointless. Who could answer the *real* questions that I had? I yearned for a teacher to instruct and guide me.

With our faith in God, my mother and I started to attend various religious and spiritual services. The good thing in Hinduism is that there are many spiritual masters teaching the same truths in their own unique way. The bad thing is—there are many spiritual masters teaching the same truths in their own unique way. It can be very confusing.

Whenever I attended a service, I would try my best to find out all I could about the master and organization or mission, if there was any. I was looking for a feeling, a conviction that this was the master for me. But, unfortunately, that didn't happen.

I continued to search for seven years, and then

moved to Toronto, Canada, after my marriage to my husband, Kumar. We had three sons in five years, and so, as you can imagine, it was an extremely busy time in our lives. My spiritual aspirations had to take a backseat for some time, but they never really went away. I jumped at every opportunity to attend spiritual talks and events. I spent as much time as I possibly could reading spiritual books, learning and growing. As the years passed, I grew more and more anxious to find my guru. Although I had no clue who he was, or where he was, I never gave up. It was a full twenty years before I finally came to deserve a guru.

The universe is constantly providing us with the right circumstances for our inner growth. But we usually only realize this in hindsight. From 1990 on, I occasionally attended lectures on Vedanta organized by the Toronto center of the Chinmaya Mission. I started taking my oldest son for the center's value-based classes for children in 1993. We continued attending irregularly with my second son until 1999. In that year, all three of the boys were ready to attend the Sunday classes together. I began attending the adult study group, which ran concurrent to the children's program in another room. We watched videotapes of spiritual discourses by Swami Chinmayananda. He had a powerful presence, even in his videos. Most of what he taught flew right over my head, but for some strange reason, it just felt good to hear him.

Sadly, my participation in the study group ended a few weeks after I joined. My oldest son, who was nine, started to complain about going to classes on Sunday mornings. The only way I could convince him to stay was by joining as a volunteer teacher in his class. Although I couldn't continue with the study group, I had a taste of what it was like, and was interested to learn more. I started reading some books on my own. As a stay-at-home mom with three playful boys full of endless energy, finding some quiet time alone wasn't easy. I often ran into the bathroom to read.

Being part of the Chinmaya children's program brought me ample new friends. There were many people who had met Swami Chinmayananda in person, attended his lectures, and had many personal anecdotes to share. I was not one of them. I had never met him in person.

In 2001 a strange thing started to happen. Whenever I heard people talk about their personal experiences with Swami Chinmayananda, something inside me would stir, and my eyes would well up in tears. It was both perplexing and embarrassing at the same time. My old yearnings for a guru surfaced.

I wondered . . . could he be the guru for me? The rational side of me denied it. He spoke great wisdom, but I didn't understand the high-level teachings. I just couldn't relate to him. But then why was I reacting emotionally to stories about him? I longed for some quiet time away from my busy duties as a mom to figure it out.

The opportunity to do that soon appeared. In 2001, Kumar and I registered the children for a two-week residential summer camp in Rochester, New York. Since it was their first time away from home, I volunteered to help in the kitchen for a week to placate my mom fears, and to settle them in. Luckily, they took to it like ducks to water. Soon afterward, I found out that there would be a two-week Chinmaya spiritual camp on meditation taking place in July 2002. It would be held at Krishnalaya, an ashram in the little town of Piercy, California. Wonder of wonders, the dates coincided perfectly with my children's summer camp dates for that year. Yes! I could finally get away by myself! I knew from their first year at camp that the boys would be fine. Kumar was totally supportive of me even though it meant sacrificing our alone time together. He knew this was important for me.

I had never been to a residential spiritual retreat and knew next to nothing about the place, or what to expect. Also, no one I knew was going. But I was excited nonetheless. The teacher would be Swami Tejomayananda, respectfully addressed as "Guruji." Guruji was Gurudev's foremost disciple and the global head of the Chinmaya Mission. I had enjoyed attending his lectures in Toronto in 2002 and was looking forward to continuing learning from him.

In the months leading up to July, even though I still felt strangely emotional when my friends spoke of Swami Chinmayananda, I continued to question whether he was the right one for me. I decided that I would find out once and for all when I got to Piercy. As I prepared to leave, however, I was torn by conflicting thoughts—"Am I doing the right thing?" "What if he's not the one?" Putting aside my fears, I flew to San Francisco airport, where I joined a busload of cheerful camp delegates who put me at ease. It was a scenic five-hour drive to Piercy. In the last hour or so, the roads were lined with breathtakingly beautiful giant redwood trees.

When we arrived, we got some terribly disappointing news—Guruji would not be there. As he was about to board the plane from Calgary, Canada, to San Francisco, he was stopped by US immigration officials and denied entry, as he didn't have the right teaching visa. He had flown to the United States to teach many times before without that particular visa, but it was just months after the September 11, 2001, attacks in New York, and security officials were being very cautious. So he was sent back to India from the Calgary airport.

The news threw me into turmoil and made me feel like an abandoned child in an unfamiliar place. Guruji was the only stabilizing factor in my trip. I was hoping to get some private time with him to share my feelings and seek his advice. But now he was not going to be there.

Piercy is a place where Swami Chinmayananda had often visited and lectured. So there was a cottage designated for him. It's a small building with a living room, a dining area, and a bedroom. The living room still had many of his books sitting on shelves. Visitors could pick up any book and sit on the sofa to read. Feeling very unsettled and wishing that Guruji was there, I reached for a book of quotes by Swami Chinmayananda. I opened it in the middle. My eyes widened in surprise as I read these words: *Avoid comparison trips! What you have now is HIS thoughtful gift. Stop crying for what you have not. You don't really need them. When needed they will be given.*[1]

I felt as if he were speaking to me.

Things soon stabilized at our camp. Swami Shantananda from the New Jersey center was asked

---

[1] Chinmayananda, *Unto Him*, 10.

to fly in and lead our studies. He is an experienced teacher who made the topic of meditation easy to understand. He arrived three days later.

We settled into a stimulating routine that started at 6 a.m. and ended at 9 p.m. There was early morning meditation and yoga, three daily lectures and lively group discussions. There were scenic walks and informal gatherings in the evenings. I was enjoying the studies and my camp mates.

Some people used to go to Swami Chinmayananda's cottage in the morning and in the evening to sit in silence on the carpeted floor of his bedroom for meditation. There was a writing desk and chair with his photo on it. The furniture was just as it had been when he was present in person. In the afternoons, the cottage was empty because people stayed in their rooms to rest or read. I, on the other hand, spent them in the cottage—mostly crying.

I would go into the bedroom and sit on the floor by his footstool and talk to him in my mind. I always had the same question: "Are you my guru?" I would ask earnestly. My heart ached for an unequivocal "yes," but it never came.

The days were passing by quickly, and we would soon be leaving the tranquil atmosphere of the ashram. My greatest fear was the thought of returning to my busy life and children without knowing if he was the one. I yearned for him to tell me. The anxiety was tearing me apart.

Then, just two days before the end of our stay, I went into his bedroom again. As usual, I sat on the floor in front of the chair. I was extremely distressed, feeling the pressure of time running out. I desperately needed an answer before I left. Looking earnestly at his photograph, I pleaded over and over again, "Please, *please* tell me if you are my guru."

Suddenly, I found myself becoming very quiet and still. I closed my eyes and found myself transported back in time. I experienced a whole life review— much like what I had read about from people who had near-death experiences. In my mind's eye, I saw my life, right from the time I was a little child, my growing-up years, my parents, the major events and people in my life including my father's death, the ensuing twenty-year search for my guru, my marriage, moving to Canada from Singapore, the children—everything—until the present moment. I realized that my life had been divinely guided and that everything had happened at the right time and just the way it was meant to be.

Then, an overpowering feeling swept over me. It was a shower of grace that infused my body from head to toe. I felt chills down my spine and goose bumps all over. With it came an undeniable knowing that Swami Chinmayananda *was indeed* my guru. *Every part of my being knew it.* I couldn't hold back my emotions. They burst out like a broken dam and I found myself sobbing. I kept repeating: *Thank you! Thank you! Thank you!* Even as I said it, I was surprised at the depth of my feelings. The gratitude was overwhelming.

As I experienced the thankfulness, I felt an intense desire to *do* something to demonstrate it. Being a trained foot reflexologist, I decided to massage his feet. And so, I pretended that he was sitting there on the chair. I gently stroked his feet and lower legs as tears of joy and relief ran down my face . . .

Meeting my guru in Swami Chinmayananda was a turning point in my life. I felt unbelievably calm and centered. Our meeting gave me strength and direction.

I say we "met" because I hadn't "found" him. He had come into my life years earlier (in 1990) and was patiently waiting for me to be ready to meet him.

You may think that since he wasn't physically present, what I experienced didn't really happen. Maybe I cooked up the whole experience in my mind because it was nearing the end of my stay in Piercy and I wanted it so much. Personally, I never doubted the deep inner knowing that Swami Chinmayananda was my guru, but I *did* doubt that he was there in the room with me.

That doubt was blown away the very next day. I came across a photograph that made me do a double take. I stopped in my tracks and my heart raced with excitement when I saw it: It was a photograph of his feet. The very *same* feet that I had "seen" while massaging the day before! The same thin legs and narrow feet—he really was there! And I really *did* massage him.

Ever since that day in Piercy, Gurudev has been a vital presence in my life. Even though I never met him in person, I meet him every day through prayer, reading, and contemplating on his teachings through his books and lectures. I stay connected with him through his disciples who continue to carry on the light that he ignited.

It doesn't matter that he's not here in person. As Ram Dass puts it: *I hang out with my guru in my heart.*[2]

---

[2] https://www.ramdass.org/ram-dass-quotes/

RESOURCES FOR FURTHER READING AND STUDY

If you've enjoyed this book and want to gain some additional tools to help you apply this new learning into your life, you can use *The Now What Workbook*. It's available as a free download at www. ManishaMelwani.com/the-now-what-workbook/

To take up a more serious study of Vedanta, you can buy some books from Chinmaya Mission and take up your own study, join a study group, or do an online course.

You'll find a large selection of books and audiovisual recordings on Chinmaya Mission's website: www.ChinmayaPublications.com.

To grasp the fundamentals of Vedanta, an excellent book for self or group study is *Self-Unfoldment* (U.S. Edition), by Swami Chinmayananda. The chapters are short, with questions and quotations for reflection at the end of each chapter. You'll find many of the ideas in this book in *Self-Unfoldment*. Group study is a very effective way to learn. You can join or form a spiritual study group of anywhere between five and fifteen members in order to learn a specific spiritual text. One person is assigned as the study group leader and facilitator. Members meet once a week for an hour and a half to read and discuss the ideas in the text. This helps to clear their doubts and to see things from different perspectives. They then go home to reflect on what they have learned.

Chinmaya study groups follow a structured and progressive scheme of study from introductory, basic, and intermediate Vedanta texts, to the advanced-level *Upanishads* and *Bhagavad Gita*. The *Upanishads* expound the knowledge of the Self in the form of dialogues between the spiritual masters and their students (see chapter 6). The *Bhagavad Gita* is the Hindu epic that presents the essence of the *Upanishads*. If you'd like to join a Chinmaya Vedanta study group, you can go to www.ChinmayaMission.com/where-we-are/ to find a group attached to a Chinmaya Mission Center near you.

The Chinmaya International Foundation (CIF) also provides excellent Vedanta courses facilitated by teachers of Vedanta. The course lessons can be sent to you via regular mail or downloaded online, or you can join a course via webinars facilitated by an *acharya* (teacher). I have personally gained tremendous growth through CIF's online Foundation Vedanta Course, Bhagavad Gita Course, and the Upanishad Course. A formal course such as this holds you accountable to your studies because you have to do a test and submit your answers at the end of each lesson. If you're ready for a daily study commitment, you may consider taking a course. The website is www.Chinfo.org.

Here's a short list of books on Vedanta that can be purchased at www.ChinmayaPublications.com. All these books are in English even though they may have titles that are in Sanskrit. You can search for the title and then click to read a description.

Basic texts on Vedanta

1. *Self-Unfoldment* (US edition)—Swami Chinmayananda
2. *The Logic of Spirituality* (with DVD)—Swami Chinmayananda
3. *Tattvabodha*—Commentary by Swami Tejomayananda

Intermediate texts on Vedanta

1. *Atmabodha*—Commentary by Swami Chinmayananda
2. *Living Vedanta (Vedanta Chintanam)*—Swami Tejomayananda
3. *Vivekachoodamani*—Commentary by Swami Chinmayananda

Advanced texts on Vedanta

1. *The Holy Geeta*—Commentary by Swami Chinmayananda
2. *Kena Upanishad*—Commentary by Swami Chinmayananda
3. *Katha Upanishad*—Commentary by Swami Chinmayananda

Books on Meditation

1. *Meditation and Life*—Swami Chinmayananda
2. *Art of Contemplation*—Swami Chinmayananda
3. *Meditation The Gateway to Freedom*—Swami Chinmayananda
4. *Meditation: A Vision*—Swami Tejomayananda

To find out more about the Chinmaya Mission, its teachers, activities, and news, you can visit www.ChinmayaMission.com

BIBLIOGRAPHY

Advayananda, Swami. "Reaching the Self—Part 1." Chinfo Channel, April 30, 2016. www.youtube.com/watch?v=frqqcuencV8

Chinmayananda, Swami. *Art of Contemplation.* Mumbai: Central Chinmaya Mission Trust, first edition 1991, reprint 1998.

———. *The Art of Man-Making: Talks on the Bhagavad Geeta.* Mumbai: Central Chinmaya Mission Trust, copyright date not shown, revised edition 2002.

———. *Atmabodha of Adi Sankaracarya: Commentary by Swami Chinmayananda.* Mumbai: Central Chinmaya Trust, copyright date not shown, revised edition 1993.

———. *Final Score: Love All!* Compiled and edited by Anjali Singh. Piercy, CA: Chinmaya Mission West, 2016.

———. *Guru: The Guiding Light.* Swami Chinmayananda et al. Piercy, CA: Chinmaya Mission West, 2009.

———. *Holy Bhagavad Gita: Talks by Swami Chinmayananda.* Directed by Bradley Boatman. Piercy, CA: Chinmaya Mission West, 1991. DVD.

———. *The Holy Geeta: Commentary by Swami Chinmayananda*. Mumbai: Central Chinmaya Mission Trust, copyright date not shown, new edition 1996.

———. *Ishavasya Upanishad: Commentary by Swami Chinmayananda*. Mumbai: Central Chinmaya Mission Trust, first edition 2001, reprint 2009.

———. *Kaivalya Upanishad: Commentary by Swami Chinmayananda*. Mumbai: Central Chinmaya Mission Trust, copyright date not shown, revised edition 1997.

———. *Katha Upanishad: A Dialogue with Death; Commentary by Swami Chinmayananda*. Mumbai: Central Chinmaya Mission Trust, copyright date not shown, reprint 2001.

———. *Kena Upanishad: Commentary by Swami Chinmayananda*. Mumbai: Central Chinmaya Mission Trust, first edition 1952, reprint 1993.

———. *Kindle Life*. Mumbai: Central Chinmaya Mission Trust, copyright date not shown, reprint 1990.

———. *The Logic of Spirituality: An Introduction to Vedanta*. Produced and directed by Bradley Boatman. Langhorne, PA: Chinmaya Publications, 1991. DVD.

———. *Mandukya Upanishad: with Gaudapada's Karika: Commentary by Swami Chinmayananda*. Mumbai:

Central Chinmaya Mission Trust, copyright date not shown, reprint 2008.

———. *Meditation and Life*. Piercy, CA: Chinmaya Publications, 1992.

———. *Mundaka Upanishad, Tale of Two Birds: Jiva and Isvara: Commentary by Swami Chinmayananda*. Mumbai: Central Chinmaya Mission Trust, 2013.

———. *Narada Bhakti Sutra, Commentary by Swami Chinmayananda*. Mumbai: Central Chinmaya Mission Trust, copyright date not shown, reprint 1999.

———. *The Penguin Swami Chinmayananda Reader*. Edited by Anita Raina Thapan. New Delhi: Penguin Books India, 2004.

———. *"Say Cheese!" Witty Wisdom by Swami Chinmayananda*. Mumbai: Central Chinmaya Mission Trust, 2004.

———. *Self-Unfoldment*. Piercy, CA: Chinmaya Mission West and Central Chinmaya Mission Trust, 2007.

———. "Spiritual Unfoldment." In *In the Company of Sages*, with Swami Tejomayananda. Piercy, CA: Chinmaya Mission West, 2005.

———. *Talks on Sankara's Vivekachudamani*. Produced and directed by Shubhra Tandon. Piercy, CA: Chinmaya Mission West. DVD.

———. *Taittiriya Upanishad*: *Commentary by Swami Chinmayananda*. Mumbai: Central Chinmaya Mission Trust, 2013.

———. *Unto Him*. CA: Chinmaya Mission West, 1994.

———. *Talks on Sankara's Vivekachoodamani*: *Commentary by Swami Chinmayananda*. Mumbai: Central Chinmaya Mission Trust, copyright date not shown, reprint 2001.

———. *We Must*: *Notes on Self-Improvement*. Mumbai: Central Chinmaya Mission Trust, copyright date not shown, reprint 1990.

Ishwarananda, Swami. *Guru Stotram*: *Commentary by Swami Ishwarananda*. Mumbai: Chinmaya Prakashan, first edition 2015.

Tapovanam, Swami. *Guidance from the Guru*. Mumbai: Central Chinmaya Mission Trust, copyright date not shown, reprint 2012.

Tejomayananda, Swami. *An Altar in Life Alters Your Life*. Mumbai: Central Chinmaya Mission Trust, first edition 2008, reprint 2013.

———. *Amrtabindu Upanishad*: *A Drop of Immortality, Commentary by Swami Tejomayananda*. Mumbai: Central Chinmaya Mission Trust, first edition 2010.

———. *Bhagavad Gita Course*. Ernakulam, Kerala, India: Chinmaya International Foundation, 2011.

———. *Discourses on the Shrimad Bhagavata*. Mumbai: Chinmaya Prakashan, first edition 2016.

———. *The Essence of Spirituality (Adhyatma Laksana)*. Mumbai: Chinmaya Prakashan, first edition 2015.

———. *Hindu Culture: An Introduction*. Piercy, CA: Chinmaya Mission West, 1993.

———. "Life Is a Gift, Living Is an Art." In *Life Is a Gift: Living Is an Art*, by Swami Tejomayananda et al. Piercy, CA: Chinmaya Mission West, 2009.

———. *Living Vedanta*. Mumbai: Chinmaya Prakashan, first edition 2014, reprint 2015.

———. *Meditation: A Vision*. Mumbai, India: Central Chinmaya Mission Trust. First edition 2003, reprint 2004.

———. *Right Thinking*. Mumbai: Chinmaya Prakshan, copyright date not shown, reprint 2014.

———. *Satsanga*. Mumbai: Chinmaya Prakshan, first edition 2012, reprint 2016.

———. *Tattvabodha of Sri Adi Sankaracarya: Commentary by Swami Tejomayananda*. Mumbai: Central Chinmaya Mission Trust, copyright date not shown, revised edition 2013.

———. *Universal Questions and Timeless Answers (Sri Rama Gita)*. Mumbai: Chinmaya Prakshan, first edition 2015.

———. *Upadesa Sara of Bhagavan Ramana Maharsi: Commentary by Swami Tejomayananda*. Mumbai:

Central Chinmaya Mission Trust, first edition 1987, reprint 2002.

———. *Upanishad Course.* Ernakulam, Kerala, India: Chinmaya International Foundation, 2017.

Tulasidasa, Gosvami. *Sri Ramacaritamanasa.* Gorakhpur, India: Gita Press, 2001.

ABOUT THE AUTHOR

Manisha Melwani is a teacher and speaker who loves sharing the spiritual wisdom of Vedanta with seekers looking for clarity and guidance in their lives. She conducts classes and workshops on numerous Vedantic topics, meditation, and stress management. Her approach is a unique blend of her Eastern roots and a Western viewpoint. She was born in Mumbai, India, raised in Singapore, and now lives in Toronto, Canada. Read her blog articles and connect with her at www.ManishaMelwani.com

For additional tools to help you
apply this new learning into your life,
download your free copy of:

The Now What Workbook

www.ManishaMelwani.com/the-now-what-workbook/

CPSIA information can be obtained
at www.ICGtesting.com
Printed in the USA
LVHW030050100919
630487LV00001B/1/P